STUDENT UNIT GUIDE

NEW EDITION

OCR AS Business Studies Unit F291

An Introduction to Business

Andy Mottershead, Judith Kelt and
Alex Grant

Philip Allan Updates, an imprint of Hodder Education, an Hachette UK company, Market Place, Deddington, Oxfordshire OX15 0SE

Orders
Bookpoint Ltd, 130 Milton Park, Abingdon, Oxfordshire OX14 4SB
tel: 01235 827827
fax: 01235 400401
e-mail: education@bookpoint.co.uk
Lines are open 9.00 a.m.–5.00 p.m., Monday to Saturday, with a 24-hour message answering service. You can also order through the Philip Allan Updates website: www.philipallan.co.uk

ISBN 978-1-4441-7185-3

First printed 2012
Impression number 5 4 3 2 1
Year 2016 2015 2014 2013 2012

Cover photo: Eric Middelkoop/Fotolia

Typeset by Integra, India

Printed in Dubai

Hachette UK's policy is to use papers that are natural, renewable and recyclable products and made from wood grown in sustainable forests. The logging and manufacturing processes are expected to conform to the environmental regulations of the country of origin.

P2089

Contents

Getting the most from this book 4

About this book 5

Content Guidance

The nature of business

The role of business 7

Stakeholders 9

Business resources 13

Finance 15

Human resources 18

Market research 22

Sampling 24

Classification of business

Ways of classifying businesses 26

Measuring the size of a business 31

Objectives 33

The market 36

Other influences

Technology 45

Social demographics 46

Ethics and corporate social responsibility 48

Questions & Answers

How to use this section 51

Case study 1: Warburtons 55

Case study 2: Innocent shifts its marketing 65

Knowledge check answers 75

Index 76

Getting the most from this book

Questions & Answers

Exam-style questions

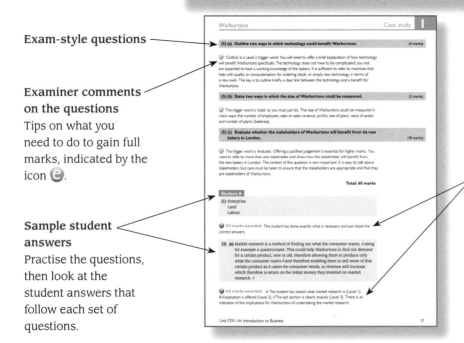

About this book

The aim of this guide is to help you to maximise your grade in the OCR examination: An Introduction to Business (F291). The information contained in the guide has been organised to mirror the textbook, *OCR AS Business Studies* (2nd edition) by Andy Mottershead, Steve Challoner and Alex Grant. This order reflects the order of the topics within the OCR specification. If you have not got a copy of the specification, it is worth downloading from the OCR website (www.ocr.org.uk), as you will then be able to tick off the topics as your revision progresses.

The guide is divided into two main sections to make your revision easier.
- **Content Guidance.** This section, which closely follows the OCR specification, outlines all the topics on which you may be tested in the examination.
- **Questions and Answers.** In this section there are two case studies for you to attempt. Each case study is very similar to what you can expect to see in your final examination. They contain the same number and type of questions as the examination to enable you to become familiar with the format of the paper. Sample A-grade answers are included to help you see what is required to reach this grade. Examiner's comments explain how each student answer is awarded marks, and highlight the exact point at which a particular level is awarded, so that you can quickly and easily adopt a similar strategy in your answers. The comments also indicate why some students' answers fall short of an A* grade.

How to revise

You have already made a good start by picking up this guide. Time spent reading each section carefully will be time well spent.
- There is no correct way to revise. Use whichever strategy and learning style best suit you.
- Find out when your examinations are and plot them on a spreadsheet or calendar. This will help you organise your revision and prioritise which subjects are to be examined first.
- Ensure you use the Content Guidance section of this guide as a checklist of all the topics you need to know.
- If it is appropriate to your learning style, write out on index cards or in a small notebook the key points in each topic. Using cards or a small notebook ensures that the amount you are trying to learn is manageable. Either format allows you to carry your notes around with you.
- For topics that you find hard to remember, it may be helpful to make a larger copy of the key words, formulae or diagrams, and stick this to your bedroom wall. A quick read-through of these before going to sleep can work wonders!
- Work on your revision in manageable periods of time. Good effective revision should be tackled in 20–30-minute sessions, rewarding yourself with a break, for example, once you have prepared a set of cards. However long your revision session is, reward yourself with the same time period for resting.
- You will need to extend this period of time when you start to practise the examination questions provided in this guide.

- Once you have finished a complete set of revision cards, you should practise examination questions to see if you can apply the information on the cards.
- Practise reading the question to note the trigger word and then write a list of the knowledge (key concepts and terms) you would include in the answer.
- Practise the levels of response in your answers. Think how the business in the case will be affected or how it might need to react (Level 3 — analysis). Try offering a justified judgement (Level 4 — evaluation).
- Ensure you practise within the time scale of the examination (1 hour). (If you are a student who is entitled to extra time, build that extra time into your practice.)
- Compare your answers with those provided in this guide and also refer to the 'Did you?' checklist below.

Did you...?

- answer the actual question — not the one you were hoping would be asked?
- note the trigger word?
- apply the right level in your answer — in context?
- note the mark allocation to ensure you used your time wisely?
- use the case to offer evidence for your views?
- offer comments on how the business would be affected or how it would react, in order to gain Level 3 marks?
- make a justified judgement for Level 4 marks?
- answer *all* the questions?

If you have answered yes to all of the above, you have definitely improved your chances of gaining an A or A*.

Content Guidance

The nature of business

The role of business

Inputs and outputs

The role of business is to convert **inputs** into **outputs**. This is achieved by using resources such as raw materials, labour, cash and entrepreneurial skills to produce goods and services that consumers require. Resources are sometimes referred to as the factors of production.

- **Land.** Land is the resource from which raw materials such as food, oil and metals are collected, and land is also the location for factories and for infrastructure such as roads.
- **Labour.** The working age is currently 16–65 for men and 16–60 for women. However, legislation has changed recently, extending the retirement age for women to 62 with the aim of achieving equality with men. Subsequent announcements have been made to extend the retirement age still further. Labour is used to perform a wide range of tasks.
- **Capital.** This is the machines used to produce goods.
- **Enterprise.** This comprises business owners or entrepreneurs — the people who have the ideas and organise the resources to produce the required goods.

For example, car production uses:
- land for the factory to assemble the cars and for some of the raw materials (e.g. iron ore) used to make the steel for the car body
- labour to help assemble the components and market the cars
- capital, which includes the robots, conveyors and assembly equipment used in the factory
- enterprise — the directors of the car business

Inputs The resources necessary to produce goods and services.

Outputs The goods and services produced from utilising inputs.

Business markets

Businesses produce a wide range of goods and services which can be classified into different markets:

- **consumer durables** — products that may be used more than once (e.g. cars, furniture and books)
- **consumer non-durables** — products that may only be used once (e.g. food and drink)
- **services** — the purchases that do not involve a good (e.g. travel, hair cuts, banking, advertising)
- **industrial** — products bought by businesses (e.g. machines, equipment necessary to produce consumer goods)

Functions of business

Any business can be divided into four main functions or departments:

- **Marketing.** The purpose of marketing is to discover the needs of consumers via market research and to satisfy this demand at a profit. Consumers will need to be informed (via advertising) of the product or service available, with incentives (sales promotion) being offered if necessary. Marketing also attempts to add value to entice consumers to purchase.
- **Finance.** This function concentrates on maximising revenues while minimising costs. It is responsible for ensuring that the business has sufficient money to keep going (**working capital**). This function is also responsible for setting budgets in order to control the business's finances.
- **Human resources management (HRM).** The HRM (or personnel) function is responsible for ensuring that the right amount and quality of employees are recruited. Once they have been recruited, it is important to look after staff to ensure they are productive. This is usually achieved by motivating the employees. Most HRM departments are responsible for ensuring that employee legislation is fulfilled.
- **Production.** The production department needs to produce sufficient goods to satisfy the demand created by the marketing department. Not only does the quantity of the products need to be right, but the quality must also be good enough to avoid rejects and complaints from consumers. In addition, it is essential to produce within budget in terms of costs, especially in a competitive market.

Constraints

Constraints are factors that may affect the running of a business. All businesses operate within an environment where there are a range of constraints. These include:

- **Competition.** The amount of competition may affect the prices that a business can charge for its goods or services. Consumers will have a choice and therefore the business will need to ensure it competes not only on price but also on service and quality.
- **Legislation.** All businesses face a wide range and ever-increasing number of laws, especially on health and safety issues.
- **The economy.** The level of activity in the economy, as shown in the trade cycle, may have a significant effect on businesses. Whether the economy is in a boom or a recession (as it was in 2009) affects the ability of consumers to spend money and therefore the level of demand for goods and services. In a recession, the level of demand will be low and therefore businesses will have to work harder in order to sell their goods. In the 2009 budget, the chancellor announced incentives to help the car industry. Cars aged 10 years and over could be scrapped for £2,000 when buying a new car.
- **Taxation.** The level of taxation, direct and indirect, affects the ability of consumers to demand goods and services. If income tax rates are increased, as they were in the 2009 budget for top income earners (rising from 40% to 50%), the disposable income of these taxpayers will fall, which in turn will reduce their ability to demand goods. The effect of changes in the rate of VAT (which in 2011 was increased from 17.5% to 20%) will depend upon the type of product that is taxed. If the product is

seen as a necessity by the consumer, the tax will not have a significant effect on the level of demand.

- **Inflation.** The level of inflation affects the ability of consumers to buy goods and services. Rising prices mean that consumers are not able to buy as many goods.
- **Social and environmental issues.** Environmental awareness is today a serious issue and one that cannot be avoided. The level of carbon emissions is now a key selling point for cars. Energy conservation is a key factor both for products in the home and for the production of goods. The reduction in the level of waste is also a high priority for businesses. Landfill is now taxed and therefore any way in which a business can reduce waste will lead to major savings in costs.

Purposes of business

Businesses serve the following purposes:
- **Source of revenue.** A business is a source of revenue for its shareholders (in the form of dividends), its employees (wages) and the government (taxation).
- **Source of employment.** Businesses provide many jobs regardless of the stage of production in which they are involved. Business is a source of employment in all stages of production: primary, secondary and tertiary.
- **Aiding the balance of payments.** Business aids the economy as it contributes to exports through its production of goods or services. As a consequence, money will come into the UK economy.
- **Adding value.** All businesses attempt to 'add value' in order to encourage consumers to purchase their goods or services at a price that is higher than the costs involved. If additional features are added to the product without excessive additional costs, the business will be successful. Changing raw materials into consumer goods adds value, as does improving the image of products in the eyes of consumers. Sometimes, very little needs to be done to add value. Putting the picture of a famous person on a product may instantly add value.

Analysis

Analysis may be attempted when, for example, constraints are being considered. Indicating how a business will be affected by a particular constraint is an obvious route to Level 3 marks.

Evaluation

Evaluation can be added by offering a justified judgement about which of the constraints is the most significant in the context of the case.

Stakeholders

Stakeholders are individuals or groups who are affected by the operations of a business, *or* individuals or groups that influence the operation of a business (see Figure 1).

Knowledge check 1

State two constraints that would affect the ability of consumers to demand products.

Examiner tip

Constraints are not always negative. It is therefore essential for you to think how a business will be affected, e.g. a road haulage company could promote itself by using low carbon emission vehicles.

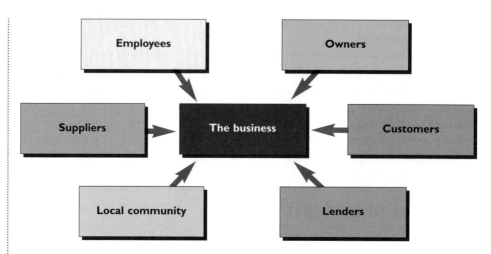

Figure 1 The stakeholders in a business

Stakeholders have differing objectives and are able to influence a business or are affected by the operation of a business to varying degrees.

Types of stakeholder

Owners

A business may be owned by one or more people. The owners or shareholders (see 'Classification of business', pp. 27–29) will benefit from a profitable business. They will want to see as much profit as possible. Making a profit may take several years and therefore stakeholders will consider the short and long term for their investments. In the short term, the owners may have to settle for no returns and even further expenditure before profits are made.

Employees

Employees are concerned about their security in terms of keeping their job. In addition, employees will want to gain the highest possible salary or wage.

Some employees will be concerned about the nature of and degree of variation within the job. Others will want the opportunity to gain promotion and have more responsibility.

Customers

The majority of customers are hoping to get value for their money. They are keen to have products of a good quality at an affordable price.

There are a growing number of customers who want the products that they buy to be ethical in terms of the carbon footprint that they leave. Sustainability is becoming an important issue and fair trade products are now being sought more frequently.

A business is more likely to respond to the needs of the customer if there is a possibility that its reputation will be damaged if it does not respond positively.

Examiner tip
Remember there may be a range of customers and therefore a range of opinions as to what is important to them. Some will prioritise ethical issues whereas low-income customers will want low prices.

Lenders

A bank is a stakeholder in many businesses. Loans are given to a business in order to finance the purchase of factories, machines and, in the short term, raw materials.

The bank will be interested in the ability of the business to repay the loan. Similarly, the bank will be encouraged if the business is profitable and wants to undertake further expansion, thus needing further loans.

Suppliers

Suppliers depend on the success or failure of the business they supply. If a business increases its sales, the suppliers will also increase their sales.

Prompt payment of suppliers will help build a good working relationship between the suppliers and the business being supplied. Reliability of supply in terms of quality and punctuality will help to maintain sales.

The community

The community may be affected both positively and negatively by the operation of a business.

The community as a whole may benefit as businesses expand and when more businesses move into the local area. More jobs may become available, which in turn means that the community will become more prosperous as people have more to spend within the community. If this is the case, the standard of the infrastructure may be improved. More leisure facilities may be supplied, and the roads may be improved (as they were when Toyota moved to the outskirts of Derby). Such improvements are known as **social benefits**.

However, the community may also have to deal with greater levels of pollution, noise and road congestion as a result of business activities. These negative effects are known as **social costs**.

The government

Although not a direct stakeholder, the government certainly can have a significant effect on the operation of a business. Similarly, businesses can have a significant effect upon the government.

- Taxation can affect demand for goods and services.
- Businesses provide employment and mean that less government money will be paid in job seeker's allowances.
- Employment means that the government will collect more tax revenue from employees (income tax and national insurance).
- Employment means that the government will also collect more revenue from taxes on consumer expenditure (VAT, excise duties, import duties).
- A successful business will probably make more profit and therefore the government will collect more revenue on company profits (corporation tax).
- It is possible that businesses may sell their goods and services abroad and will therefore help the government by increasing exports and therefore helping the balance of payments.

> **Examiner tip**
> When considering the most important stakeholders, always take into account the business given in the question, e.g. shareholders will be particularly interested in a business whose main objective is raising profits.

- The government spends money on schools, roads and hospitals, which can affect the attractiveness of an area. People who are thinking of moving to a new job will carefully consider the facilities of an area before moving.

Roles of the state

The state has a considerable effect on the operations of a business because it has many roles.

The state as a consumer

The state will buy from businesses in order to provide for the population. The health service requires medicines and equipment for its hospitals, roads need to be built and equipment is required for the armed forces.

The state as a supplier

The state provides a wide range of services for the benefit of the community:
- health
- education
- social services (benefits)
- roads
- armed forces

The majority of the above are referred to as **merit goods**.

The state as a regulator

The state passes laws (legislation) to control the behaviour of businesses when dealing with consumers (consumer protection), employees (recruitment and dismissal) and how businesses behave towards each other (competition).

The state as an economic regulator

Attempting to control the economy is a major role of the state. The government will use taxation and government expenditure to try to control:
- inflation
- employment
- growth
- the balance of payments

These areas are also influenced by interest rates, which are determined by the Monetary Policy Committee of the Bank of England.

Conflicts between stakeholders

Given the wide range of stakeholders, it is inevitable that each will have its own priorities. For example, a business will want to keep costs down in order to make sufficient profit to satisfy its shareholders, while employees will want to ensure they have sufficient wages and job security.

Environmentalists do not want another runway at Heathrow airport, but the government is keen to ensure that Heathrow remains a major airport hub. Closing a heavily polluting factory may please the local community, but employees will lose their jobs.

Knowledge check 2

State three ways in which the state may affect a business.

Social and ethical issues concern the state because, for example, it taxes alcohol and tobacco while increasing the opening hours of public houses. Landlords of the public houses will be pleased at the extended opening hours, but the local residents may not like the noise taking place in their neighbourhood for more hours of the day and night. Landlords may not like the increased taxes on alcohol, but as a result the government will have more revenue to spend on the health service, which benefits patients.

Analysis

Showing how a particular stakeholder will benefit or suffer in the context of the case is the obvious route to Level 3 marks. Alternatively, you could show how the business or stakeholders of the business will react to the information given in the case.

Evaluation

Comparing how a range of stakeholders will be affected and then making a justified judgement about which group of stakeholders will be affected the most will lead to Level 4 marks. It is just as valid to justify why a particular group of stakeholders will not be affected.

Knowledge check 3

State three stakeholders who may be in conflict if a business introduces a wage freeze.

Business resources

Businesses need a range of resources in order to survive and prosper.

Essential resources

The resources required to run any business are often listed as:
- an effective business plan
- employees
- finance
- products/services that are unique

A business plan

A business plan helps the owners to plan what is required (what needs to be done, how and when).

The plan normally includes the business's strategic and tactical objectives. It will include its targets, details of its finance and how the business is to operate. The plan will need to be effectively communicated to the employees of the business.

The business plan is a useful document when finance is required. A bank will be interested to see how organised the business is, and the plan can be used to show the bank that careful thought has been given to how the business is to operate and achieve its objectives. The bank is more likely to lend money to a business if a detailed plan exists.

Business plan A report that outlines strategies for a business.

Examiner tip

If asked to suggest how useful a business plan is for a business, try to include both its positive and negative aspects (e.g. it may be far too optimistic or lack sufficient research).

Employees

Employees need to have the right skills for the business. They need to be trained appropriately and to be led by effective managers.

Managers need to be able to coordinate, motivate, plan and control their employees in order to get the best out of the workforce.

Finance

Finance is necessary in order to fund the buildings and equipment needed to operate the business. Funds will also be needed to meet the everyday bills of the business, which include paying the wages of employees, buying the raw materials needed to produce the goods and paying the utility bills (gas, electricity).

Ensuring that there are sufficient funds to pay these bills when they fall due is a crucial task for the business's finance department.

The right product or service

Knowledge check 4

State four likely essential resources that a business will need.

Selling the right products is essential to the survival of the business. Market research can be used to ascertain what the consumers want. In many markets the level of competition is very high, and therefore if a business can have a unique selling point (USP), it is more likely to survive and prosper.

What makes a successful business?

The items shown in Figure 2 clearly demonstrate that many factors may affect the success of a business.

The success of a business can be measured in terms of:
- the amount of profit made
- the market share of the business
- the level of sales
- its number of customers and repeat customers

A business with high and increasing levels of these criteria may be considered successful.

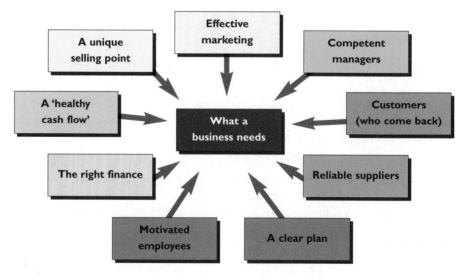

Figure 2 The requirements of a successful business

Why do some businesses fail?

Businesses fail all too easily. In particular, a large percentage of new businesses fail for one or more of the following reasons:

- a poor business plan (or no real business plan)
- a lack of professional advice
- poor finances or lack of finance
- a lack of market research
- an inability to change with the times (a lack of adaptability)
- a poor product or service
- an inability to grow effectively

Knowledge check 5
State three reasons why a business may fail.

Analysis

You should be able to suggest how a business will be affected if it does not have sufficient resources. For example:

- If the business has insufficient finance, it will not be able to afford to give its employees a pay rise and therefore it may lose some employees to more highly paid jobs.
- This in turn will mean that the business has to spend more money on recruiting and training new staff.

Evaluation

You should be able to make a justified judgement about which of the resources will be most important to a business in a given situation. For example, given that the business is keen to expand, it will need additional employees and additional finance to pay for the expansion. The existing staff could be paid overtime, whereas there is no alternative to finding the additional finance because without it none of the expansion programme can take place.

Finance

Money is an essential resource for all businesses. Finance is required for:

- starting a business
- buying raw materials
- paying utility bills
- wages
- capital equipment
- marketing

Finance to meet the day-to-day needs of a business is called **working capital** (i.e. money to keep the business working).

The sources of finance are usually divided into categories. Which source of finance is used will depend upon the amount required and why it is needed.

Capital equipment
Anything that is used in the production and delivery of a good or service to a final consumer, e.g. a robot used to weld car parts together.

Knowledge check 6
Give two day-to-day uses for working capital.

Internal and external sources of finance

Internal finance is when a business generates its own finance through retained profit, selling assets and trade credit.

External finance is obtained from outside of the business, in the form of overdrafts, loans, mortgages, shares and debentures, all of which will require some form of repayment.

Short-term finance

In order to keep the business working, cash (working capital) is needed. If there is insufficient capital available within the business because more money is going out of the business (outflows) than coming into the business (inflows), then the business will need to borrow cash.

Overdraft

Most current accounts have an automatic overdraft level built in. However, a business can negotiate with the bank for a larger limit depending upon its circumstances.

The overdraft is flexible and interest is only paid on the amount actually overdrawn and for the time it is overdrawn. An overdraft is used to improve the cash flow of the business and not to buy capital equipment.

Short-term loan

A short-term loan is usually used to purchase specific machinery or to ensure that a sufficient amount of raw materials is available. When the loan is taken out, it is credited to an account of the business. The business repays the loan and the interest charged over an agreed period of time. Unlike an overdraft, the loan is for a specified amount for a fixed period of time.

Trade credit

This is when a business is allowed to take delivery of supplies without having to pay for them straight away. By having a period of credit, a business can use the supplies and possibly sell its goods before it has to pay for the supplies used. This helps the cash flow of the business, as it is delaying an outflow from the business. It is really a form of borrowed finance without having to pay interest.

Factoring

A business is able to sell its debts to a factoring company in exchange for cash. The business may have several businesses that owe it money. To increase the level of cash immediately, rather than waiting to be paid by its debtors, the business can sell the debt to a factoring company, which will give the business a percentage of the debt (possibly 90%) immediately. The factoring company will keep the other 10% as a charge for its immediate payment to the business.

Examiner tip

It is important to remember that cash flow and working capital are more important to a business than profitability. Firms cannot survive for long if they do not have money flowing into them.

Medium-term finance

Medium-term loan

The arrangements for such a loan are the same as for a short-term loan. The loan will be for an agreed period of time, usually between 3 and 10 years. The level of interest paid on the loan will depend upon both the actual amount to be borrowed and the length of the loan. The interest rate is normally fixed for the period of the loan.

This type of loan is more likely to be used to help the business expand by buying additional premises and new machines. It may also be used to replace old machinery.

Hire purchase

This method enables a business to pay for a machine by instalments over a given period of time. The goods do not become the property of the business until the last payment has been made. Hire purchase enables the business to spread the cost over time.

Leasing

This source is similar to hire purchase in that the costs are spread over time. However, the business does not own the goods as leasing is a form of rent. The benefits to the business are not only the spreading of the cost, but also the fact that any faults occurring have to be paid for by the leasing company.

Knowledge check 7

What is the main difference between hire purchase and leasing?

Long-term finance

Long-term loan

This type of loan is normally for large amounts, which are necessary to fund the purchase of very expensive machinery or premises that will last for many years. Due to the great expense, it is necessary to spread the cost over a very long period.

Loans for buildings are often referred to as **mortgages** and could run for between 15 and 25 years. For such large loans, as with medium-term loans, banks require significant security including the deeds to the land or other saleable assets.

Shares

Issuing shares (equitable finance) is a source of finance that enables a business to raise significant amounts of money without needing to repay the amount invested. Instead, the business will offer **dividends** (a proportion of the profits) to the shareholders on an annual basis (this depends on the level of the profits and how much the company decides to pay). A private limited company is restricted in terms of whom it can offer shares to, whereas for a public limited company, shares can be made available to the general public.

Retained profits

This is a very cheap form of credit, as it does not incur any debt. However, using retained profit may mean that more profit has to be kept in the firm and that less is available for distribution to shareholders in the form of dividends.

Examiner tip

Make sure that you understand the difference between a shareholder and a stakeholder. Students often misread and confuse the two terms in exam situations.

Additional sources of finance

Government grants are available to businesses and are usually obtained from the Department for Business, Innovation and Skills (BIS). These include:

- the Enterprise Finance Guarantee (EFG) scheme
- assistance via Local Enterprise Partnerships
- EU grants

In addition, further assistance may be gained from venture capitalists and business angels.

Which type of finance?

The type of finance used will depend on a range of factors:

- the type and size of the business
- security (assets)
- existing internal funds
- existing levels of debt
- relationship with the banks and other financial institutions
- time period for repayments

Analysis

Questions asking you for analysis will allow you to indicate the consequences for the business of using a particular type of finance. The implications may be related to the effect it will have on the business (more debt or increased costs) or how it will allow the business to expand and therefore achieve its objectives. They may also allow you to think about the consequences for the various stakeholders of the business.

Evaluation

Evaluative comments are likely to be related to making a judgement about which is the most appropriate method of finance for the given business and what it is trying to achieve. Remember to use the context of the case and the type of business when considering the most appropriate method of finance.

Human resources

Human resource management (HRM) is concerned with employees. Ensuring that employees are well looked after should benefit the business as a whole.

There are two key elements to HRM:

- recruitment
- training

Each is vital if the business is to prosper.

Examiner tip

Think carefully about the size and nature of the business and the proposed use for the money, before suggesting a source of finance. Make sure that your suggestion is appropriate. For example, issuing shares is not appropriate for a sole trader.

Recruitment

In order to recruit the right staff, careful thought needs to be given to the various stages of the recruitment process.

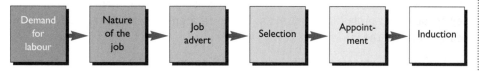

Figure 3 Stages of recruitment

Demand for labour

How much labour is required by a business depends upon:
- the demand for the products of the business
- the amount of machinery that could be used instead of labour
- the cost of the labour

How important each of the above is depends upon the nature of the product or service involved. A hotel requires more labour than an automated production business.

If the scale of the production process is large, it is more likely that machines will be used to produce the goods, and therefore the demand for labour will be considerably smaller.

If the cost of labour is high, the business may try to manage with fewer employees in order to save money.

Nature of the job

This relates to the actual tasks that need to be performed. A job description is needed, containing:
- job title
- line manager
- what the job entails

Sometimes the job description includes a list of the working conditions, such as:
- number of hours
- number of days holiday
- additional benefits (e.g. company car or staff dining room)

Once a job description has been drawn up, a **person profile** or **job specification** can be prepared. This lists the qualities and qualifications for an ideal person to fit the job description, including:
- qualifications (e.g. NVQs, degree)
- experience required
- qualities, such as an ability to motivate others
- good ICT skills

Job advert

How a job is advertised depends upon whether the post is to be filled internally or externally.

Labour/capital intensive Firms that use large amounts of labour are called labour intensive and those that use large amounts of capital are called capital intensive.

Knowledge check 8

Give an example of a business that is (a) labour intensive and (b) capital intensive.

Based on the job description and the job specification, an advert will need to be placed in an appropriate medium. Which medium is used depends upon the nature of the job, the cost of placing the advert, and the ability of various media to attract the 'right' type of person.

The most popular media used for job advertisements are national and local newspapers and professional journals. However, a growing number of adverts are being placed on the internet.

Most job advertisements try to include information on both the job specification and the person profile in an attempt to ensure that those who apply for the post advertised are serious candidates with the appropriate qualities.

The selection process

Candidates normally submit a CV (curriculum vitae) along with a completed application form. In addition, some posts require a letter of application.

Once the application has been sifted, a short-list is made. The short-listed candidates are usually invited to attend an interview, although what actually occurs will vary depending upon the advertised post.

The selection process may consist of some or all of the following techniques:
- aptitude testing, in which a candidate is set a particular task or role to deal with that may be encountered in the actual post
- interview panels, asking a range of open and closed questions
- psychometric tests, which are used to assess the personality of the candidate

The use of interviews alone is declining, as this method of selection may not be as reliable as once thought. The size of the interview panel, and the inability of the panel to ask the 'right' questions and interpret the answers, have brought the reliability of interviews into question.

Selection of the 'right' candidate has to be made within the law. There are laws to prevent selection procedures that discriminate on the basis of sex, age, culture and disability.

Appointment

Knowledge check 9

What information may be listed in a person profile?

On appointment, the employee must be given a **contract of employment** within 2 months of starting work (Employment Rights Act 1996). The contract must contain the following details:
- job name/title
- employment location
- hours of work
- rate of pay
- when payment is made
- holidays
- entitlements such as holidays and pensions
- terms of notice (e.g. 1 month)

Induction

In many jobs, there is an induction programme to help new employees settle in and be more comfortable and content in the job.

Knowing clearly what the ethos of the business is and how it operates should help to keep the retention levels of the business high, and therefore save the business additional expenditure on further recruitment.

Training

Training will help the business to maximise the productivity and efficiency of its employees. Providing training ought to help increase employee motivation.

There are two main types of training: on-the-job and off-the-job. Which is used by the business will depend upon:
- the size of the business
- the cost of training
- the skills of the trainers and the trainees
- the time available

Even a single business may vary in its use of on- and off-the-job training.

On-the-job training takes place within the business. As a consequence, it is usually more convenient and cheaper. On-the-job training in-house takes less time as travel is not necessary. It can also take place to suit the business rather than when the courses are offered.

How effective on-the-job training is will largely depend upon the skill of the trainer. If the business has skilled trainers, they will be able to pass on the skills required in a manner that is appropriate to the business.

Off-the-job training is undertaken by an outside agency, and the timing and actual content of the courses will be tailored to satisfy a range of people. Therefore the business will have less control over what training takes place and how it is implemented.

Off-the-job training is usually more expensive. However, it does allow a business to use experts in particular skills that it may not have itself.

Although training may be expensive and a better-qualified employee may require higher wages, the returns are usually worth the expenditure involved because, if a business is to prosper, it must invest in all of its resources, including labour.

Analysis

Analysis can be undertaken when considering the costs and benefits of training. Highlighting the consequences for the business of spending money on its workforce, suggesting the consequences of not training employees, or highlighting the benefits of either on-the-job or off-the-job training are all possible routes to a Level 3 mark.

Examiner tip

It is important to remember that recruitment, induction and training will always be a significant cost for a business. Firms that have high labour turnover may well be getting the recruitment process wrong.

Evaluation

Evaluation will normally be undertaken by making a justified judgement about which type of training will be the most appropriate for a given business. Using the clues in the case as to the budget of the business, the skills of its workforce and what is required in terms of training are all factors that will influence this judgement.

Market research

Market research is concerned with the collection of information that will help a business to provide consumers with what they want. It helps the business to understand its market and its consumers by:
- describing the market — trends, share, performance etc.
- explaining the market — why the trends have occurred and why consumers liked the products
- predicting changes in the market — the consequences of the business changing its prices, of competitors' actions, or of introducing a new model
- exploring consumer reactions in the future — where to sell, how to promote and getting the price right for the consumers

Quantitative and qualitative market research

Quantitative market research concentrates on numbers — for example, on how many goods are sold and what trends there are in the market.

Qualitative market research concentrates on reasons for the data. It often involves people's opinions rather than how many of them think or act in a certain way. Such information is very useful when formulating promotional policies.

Primary and secondary data

It is important to distinguish the two types of data obtained by market research. Primary data are data collected for the specific use of the business, whereas secondary data are data that have already been collected by someone else for another purpose, and will therefore not be as specific.

Methods of primary research

Primary (field) research can involve any of the following methods:
- **Interviews.** These allow a business to concentrate on a relatively small number of individuals and therefore collect detailed information. An interview allows the respondents to answer in more detail in their own way, rather than just responding to specific questions.
- **Surveys (questionnaires).** These ask a series of pre-set questions and are useful for gaining large amounts of information. Questionnaires ensure a standardised response, making analysis easier. Surveys can be conducted face to face, by post, on the telephone or via the internet.

OCR AS Business Studies

- **Observations.** A lot can be learned simply by watching consumers' behaviour. This is a good technique for studying the behaviour of younger consumers who would not necessarily be able to respond to surveys or interviews. Examples are observing how children play with toys and observing the shopping habits of consumers.
- **Test panels.** These are often used before the launch of a product or after a regional launch but before a national launch. The panels may be asked to taste food, smell perfume or trial a new washing powder.

Methods of secondary research

Methods of secondary (desk) research can be divided into internal and external methods.

Internal methods analyse the following:
- **Company sales figures.** Results over time can be used to establish the trend of sales.
- **Customer data.** Information can be collected on customers by using data gained from retail loyalty cards and databases generated from customer orders, to establish their buying habits.

External methods analyse the following:
- **Competitors.** Information about competitors can be checked via their websites and catalogues.
- **Market research data.** Information that has been collected by companies such as Mintel provides valuable information on the markets in which a business operates. This saves it valuable time and costs.
- **Internet.** A wide range of data can be found on the internet.
- **Trade publications.** A growing source of vital information is presented by specialist publications for specific markets.
- **Newspapers and magazines.** The press offers information about the state of the economy and world markets, together with general news that may affect the selling climate for businesses.
- **Government data.** The government issues a vast range of data, including population figures, social trends and economic data.

Analysis

Showing the benefits for a business of undertaking market research is an obvious route for analytical marks.

Evaluation

Evaluative comments are likely to be related to the selection of appropriate methods of research, judged in the context of the case and the actual business. For a small business, research is likely to be secondary as it is cheaper. Any primary research that is undertaken will be collected using convenience sampling in order to keep costs down.

Knowledge check 10

How might a soap powder manufacturer undertake market research to ascertain the demand for a new stain remover?

Knowledge check 11

Suggest two methods of secondary research that could be undertaken before opening a new Indian restaurant in a small market town.

Sampling

The significance of sampling

Sampling is a cost-effective method of collecting information. Although it would be more accurate to collect information from everyone, it would be too time-consuming and expensive. Therefore sampling is used in order to reduce the costs.

Sampling methods

It is important to try to ensure that the people approached are representative of those targeted. The sample size may be crucial. Obviously, the larger the sample size, the more reliable the information.

The sampling methods described below are the most often used.

Random sampling

As the name implies, in random sampling there is an equal chance of anyone being selected. In order to achieve this, every nth person is used. However, if a random sample for a particular group was required, then drawing lots would be appropriate.

If the population is very large, random samples would be expensive and therefore an element of convenience sampling (see below) could be used.

Stratified sampling

When a specific group that has particular characteristics needs to be surveyed, a stratified sample is appropriate. A typical stratified sample could be based on gender or age, or have a similar characteristic such as hair colour.

Cluster sampling

This involves selecting a small group that represents a much larger group. Collecting information about how people will vote often uses cluster sampling to save time and costs.

Systematic sampling

This is sampling by formula. Using a set approach which involves selecting every hundredth person, for example, suggests that the sampling is fair and therefore not subject to any bias.

Convenience sampling

This type of sampling is one of the most frequently used. This is because it is a quick and convenient way to collect data. The sample of people asked is more likely to be local (saving time) or appear roughly to fit the desired group. They may even be friends of the collector, who knows they will answer the required questions. Convenience sampling therefore lacks accuracy and is less reliable.

Examiner tip
Ensure that you understand clearly exactly what sampling is. It is deciding on the group of people who will be questioned in any market research investigation. It is not the research itself.

Quota sampling

This type of sampling concentrates on gaining enough information. It selects individuals to mirror the characteristics of the total population or required segment. The key consideration is to gain a sufficient number of people in each segment required. For example, if 25% of the population being studied is over 50 years old, then the quota should reflect this.

Factors to consider when selecting a sample technique

Much will depend on the size of the business and the information that is required. No one method of sampling is perfect, so it might be necessary to use a combination. It is important to weigh up:

- the need for reliable information
- the cost of collection
- the budget available
- how quickly the information can be collected
- how up to date the information is

Analysis

Analysis could focus on the reliability of sampling techniques. If a random sample is used, it could be less effective as there is no guarantee that the people you want to survey will be included. This could therefore mean that the business has wasted a lot of money and has not collected any information that will help it to provide consumers with what is required.

Evaluation

Making a justified judgement about which methods of sampling are the most appropriate for a given business is an obvious route to a Level 4 answer. This will depend upon the actual business in the case and application of the factors to consider when selecting a method of sampling.

Knowledge check 12

Suggest an appropriate type of sampling method for a new gym to use to ascertain the level of interest from potential customers for a new yoga class.

Summary

- Inputs are used to produce outputs.
- All businesses are faced with constraints.
- Stakeholders are individuals or groups that are affected by a business or influence its actions.
- Businesses require a business plan, employees, finance and products or services that are unique.
- A business may fail if it lacks one or more of these essential resources.
- Finance for day-to-day activity is working capital.
- Finance can be raised internally and externally.
- Short-term sources of finance include overdrafts, loans, trade credit and factoring.

- Medium-term sources of finance include loans, hire purchase and leasing.
- Long-term sources of finance include share issue and retained profit.
- Demand for labour depends on demand for the final good or service, the availability of machinery and the relative cost of labour.
- The first stage in recruiting labour is to write a job description.
- Job adverts need to attract suitable employees and discourage unsuitable applicants.

(Summary continues over the page)

Summary

(Continued)

- The selection process might include interviews, tests and group activities.
- Once appointed the new employee will need induction and training.
- Market research involves collecting information to enable firms to give consumers the goods and services they want.
- Qualitative research involves collecting information about consumers. Quantitative research involves collecting numerical information about the market.

- Primary research is new research and is usually expensive to undertake. The business may need to use a specialist firm. The advantage of this type of research is that it is up to date and specific to the business.
- Secondary research involves using existing information. It is usually cheaper to undertake, but it may be out of date or may not be applicable to the business.
- Sampling is deciding on which group of people are going to be questioned or surveyed as part of a market research investigation. The main types of sampling are random, convenience, stratified and cluster.

Classification of business

Ways of classifying businesses

Businesses can be classified in the following ways:
- by the stage of production in which the business is involved
- according to whether they are private companies or controlled by the government
- by the legal structure of the business

Stages of production

All products pass along the chain of production. At each stage of this process, value is added by the actions of the businesses involved. For example, a farmer takes seed and grows it into grain. This is then milled and turned into flour. The flour is taken by the baker and turned into bread by adding other ingredients. At this point the bread can be sold to the consumer or it can be passed on to a supermarket or café and used in making sandwiches. At each stage of this process, value is added to the product by the producer.

Sectors of the economy

Business activity can be classified into three sectors:
- **Primary sector.** Businesses in the primary sector are concerned with the extractive industries. These include farming, fishing, forestry, mining and oil and gas drilling.
- **Secondary sector.** Businesses in the secondary sector are concerned with manufacture — turning raw materials into semi-finished and finished products. Examples are car manufacture, oil refining and making clothes. The construction industry is also part of the secondary sector. The decline that has taken place in the secondary sector in recent decades is known as **deindustrialisation**.
- **Tertiary sector.** This is the service sector and has no tangible, finished product. The tertiary sector includes travel, banking and medical and education services.

Knowledge check 13

Give an example of a business at the primary, secondary and tertiary stages of production.

Private and public ownership

Businesses can be classified into those in the private sector of the economy and those in the public sector.

Private sector businesses include:
- sole traders
- partnerships
- private limited companies (Ltd)
- public limited companies (plc)

Public sector businesses comprise:
- those owned and controlled by central government
- those owned and controlled by local government

Private sector businesses

The term entrepreneur is often used to describe the person who runs a business in the private sector; it means the risk taker. This person is risking his or her money to set up the business; in return for this risk they will take the profit.

Sole traders

A sole trader is the simplest form of business organisation. The sole trader makes all the decisions, although others may be employed. The owner and the business are the same entity.

Disadvantages of sole trading

- The sole trader is responsible for all the debts. His or her personal possessions and money can be taken to settle the debts of the business. This is called unlimited liability.
- Sole traders have to be 'jacks of all trades'. They have to order stock, keep the books, organise marketing, set prices etc.
- It can be difficult to raise finance for growth.
- It is difficult to take time off and sickness can cause major problems for the business.
- The business ceases to exist when the owner dies.

Partnerships

If two or more people run a business together, they are partners. The law requires a minimum of two and a maximum of 20 partners. A partnership is not a legal entity; as with sole traders, there is unlimited liability.

The **deed of partnership** is a legal document drawn up by the partners to lay down the rules under which the partnership will be run. It sets out such matters as:
- how much money each partner puts in
- how much profit each takes out
- how the responsibilities are shared
- the arrangements for absence and sickness
- how decisions will be made

Examiner tip

Be careful not to confuse public sector businesses (government owned) with public limited companies (plcs).

- how new partners will be chosen and employed
- how the partnership will be dissolved

Advantages of partnerships

- A partnership is easy to establish.
- New partners can bring in more capital.
- Work and responsibility are shared.
- Partners can specialise in what they do best or what they enjoy.
- Losses are shared.
- The financial state of the business can be kept private.

Disadvantages of partnerships

- There is still unlimited liability. However, 'sleeping partners', who simply contribute money and take a share of the profit, have limited liability.
- Decision making is slower with more people involved.
- The restriction to 20 partners still limits the capital that can be raised.
- Profits are shared as well as losses.
- There is no continuity.

Limited companies

The main features of limited companies are as follows:

- **Incorporation.** A company exists in its own right. It can be taken to court and be sued. Those who own a company, the shareholders, are not the same as those who run it, the directors.
- **Shares.** Companies can raise capital through the issue of shares. Each shareholder owns part of the company. Investors buy shares for the returns they earn (dividend) and in the hope of making a profit if they sell their shares.
- **Limited liability.** All shareholders have limited liability. This means that if the company goes into liquidation, the shareholders can only lose the value of their shares. They are not personally liable for the losses of the company.

Limited companies can be either private limited companies (Ltd) or public limited companies (plc).

Private limited companies

The main features of Ltd companies are:

- They are often family businesses.
- Shareholders must be sought by personal approach.
- The business will have 'Company Limited' (often 'Ltd') after its name.
- The company needs to file a limited set of accounts with Companies House, so some information must be disclosed.
- The owners of the business can sell the business, but it cannot be involuntarily taken over.

Public limited companies

- These are much larger organisations than Ltds; they have 'plc' after their name.
- Their shares can be traded on the Stock Exchange.

Knowledge check 14

Why is it better, although not necessary, for a partnership to have a deed of partnership?

Examiner tip

Make sure that you refer to sole traders and partnerships as businesses or firms. They are *not* companies.

Examiner tip

Limited liability is the most important and valuable characteristic of a company. Make sure that you can define it accurately.

- Anyone can buy the shares and their sale can be advertised publicly.
- A plc can be taken over if an investor gains 51% of the shares.
- The plc must disclose a full set of its accounts each year to its shareholders.
- Shareholders elect a board of directors.
- Shareholders are entitled to attend the annual general meeting (AGM) and vote; they can question the directors at the AGM.
- Voting at AGMs is one vote per share.

Advantages of limited companies

- They are able to raise large amounts of capital by selling shares.
- Limited liability is a huge benefit.
- Investors regard them as more secure than sole traders.
- Continuity — the business does not cease to exist if a shareholder dies because the shares are transferable.

Disadvantages of limited companies

- Setting up a company is expensive.
- There are documents to be filled in to set up a company, so the process is time-consuming. These documents are the **Memorandum of Association**, describing the nature of the company and its business, and the **Articles of Association**, which deal with the running of the company.
- Running a company is more complex than being a sole trader or a partnership.
- Directors have legal responsibilities such as filing accounts.

Limited liability partnerships

Limited liability partnerships (LLPs) first became legal in 2001.
- They combine features of a partnership with those of a limited company.
- The owners are called members, not partners.
- LLPs have to disclose information by filing accounts at Companies House.

Franchises

Franchises have the following characteristics:
- A franchise is a business with a well-known brand name.
- The franchisee sets up the business using this brand name.
- Franchisees can have unlimited liability if they are set up as a sole trader or partnership and limited liability if they are set up as a company.
- A fee is paid for use of the brand name.
- Examples of franchises are McDonald's, Subway and Body Shop.

The public sector

The main features of public sector companies are as follows:
- Central and local government use the money that is collected through various forms of taxation to provide services and benefits for the UK population.
- National government provides services such as education, healthcare and pensions.
- Local government provides services such as swimming pools, street lights and refuse collection.

> **Examiner tip**
> Learn the differences between private and public limited companies carefully as this is a common question on exam papers.

> **Knowledge check 15**
> Give two benefits of running a franchise business.

Examiner tip

Public spending and the public sector refer to the government sector.

- These organisations are not profit-making.
- There are some similarities to the private sector. Managers in the public sector are expected to provide a high-quality service like other businesses. They are also expected to keep tight control of finance.

Privatisation

Privatisation is the process by which government passes a public sector business into the private sector by selling shares in it. It then becomes a public limited company. The reverse process, by which government purchases a business, is called **nationalisation**. Some UK banks were nationalised during the financial crisis of 2008/09.

The purpose of privatisation is to make businesses more competitive within the market. Privatisation also encourages new firms to enter the market. For example, the privatisation of BT opened up the market to many new businesses and encouraged competition in the telecommunications industry.

Advantages of privatisation are:
- greater efficiency
- more competition

Disadvantages of privatisation are:
- some industries may be sold off too cheaply
- private sector businesses may be less socially responsible

E-business

Most businesses now use the internet in some way. The key features of e-business are:
- It may reduce the overheads for a business and remove the need for large premises.
- Home working can be used.
- The business is open 24/7.
- To be successful the technology must be reliable.
- The payment system needs to be secure or customers will stop buying on the internet.
- Websites need to be user-friendly and fast.
- Distributors must follow up sales with efficient delivery.
- Although internet access is now widespread, it is not universal.

Analysis

Analysis is likely to involve discussion of the most appropriate type of business organisation for a particular firm. It is important to remember that only very large firms will have the means and the opportunity to become public limited companies and have their shares quoted on the Stock Exchange.

The analysis could involve the discussion of what the costs and benefits will be of choosing to be a sole trader, partnership, franchise or company.

Evaluation

This could be achieved by choosing the best option for organising the business and explaining why it is the most appropriate. You could also evaluate by ranking the alternatives in terms of suitability.

Measuring the size of a business

It is common to hear statements about businesses dominating particular sectors. There are different ways in which the size of a business can be measured. The method chosen will usually depend on the nature of the business.

How can the size of a business be measured?

There are several different ways of measuring the size of a business.

Number of employees

- In most cases, large businesses employ large numbers of people. But this is not always true. Businesses like electricity generation firms are capital intensive and employ relatively few people for their size.
- How are part-time employees counted? This is significant for businesses with a high proportion of part-time staff, such as the catering industry.
- In the UK, a firm of fewer than 50 employees is regarded as small and one with more than 250 as large.

Number of factories or shops

- For some businesses, it makes more sense to count the number of production units or outlets.
- In the banking sector, one measure of size that is often used is the number of high-street branches.

Turnover and profit levels

- **Turnover** is the value of total sales revenue.
- **Profit** is the difference between sales revenue and costs.
- A high turnover is often associated with a large business. However, it is possible to find a successful business with only small premises and a huge turnover. An example is a one-person internet business with a profitable niche in the market.
- Sometimes large businesses find themselves in situations where they are making very little profit or even a loss.

Stock market value

- The value of a company can be measured by multiplying the number of its shares by the price of the shares on the Stock Exchange.
- There are problems with this method. If the price of the shares falls, it reduces the value of the company, despite the fact that there has been no change in its actual size. This situation was apparent with the fall in the value of bank shares during the credit crunch.

> **Examiner tip**
> Think about the nature of the business in the question to help you decide the best way of measuring its size.

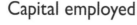
Capital employed

- Capital employed is the total value of the business's assets. If this is a high figure, the business is likely to be large.
- Using capital employed to judge the size of a business has problems with regard to the value of property assets. A business in London and a business in the northeast, of similar size, would have different values attached to their land and property, and this would affect their capital employed valuation.

Knowledge check 16

What would be the best way to measure the size of a travel agent business?

Analysis

Analysis can be achieved by discussing whether or not data on the size of firms make it possible to judge their relative size. As shown above, it is almost impossible to use any of the methods and say definitely that a business is large or small.

Evaluation

Evaluation could be achieved by weighing up how accurate information on size is likely to be in allowing the observer to judge the size of a business. It is also possible to rank different methods of judging size in terms of how useful they might be for a particular sector of the economy. For example, the number of shops might be most appropriate for a bakery chain, whereas the number of employees or turnover might be more appropriate for a car manufacturer.

Summary

- Businesses can be classified by their stage of production, their legal status or whether they are in the public or private sector.
- The stages of production are primary, secondary and tertiary.
- Primary production is at the extraction stage, e.g. fishing. Secondary production is at the manufacturing stage, e.g. chocolate making. The tertiary sector is the service sector, e.g. retail outlets.
- Public sector firms are controlled by the government and owned by the nation. Private sector firms are owned by private individuals.
- A sole trader is the smallest type of legal status for a business. It is owned by one individual and the owner and the business are the same legal entity.
- A partnership is a group of people running a business together. They do not need a deed of partnership but it is beneficial to have one.
- Limited companies can be public (plcs) or private.
- Plcs are quoted on the Stock Exchange and have to disclose complete sets of accounts and other information. They are expensive to set up.

- Private limited companies only have to disclose limited information. They are usually owned by family, friends or small groups of colleagues.
- The main advantage of being a company of either type is that the shareholders have limited liability. This means that if the business fails they can only lose money put into shares.
- The public sector is the government sector.
- The size of a business can be measured in a variety of ways. The method used to judge size should be appropriate to the type of business:
  - Business size can be measured by the number of employees a firm has.
  - Turnover and profit can also be used.
  - For businesses in the tertiary sector, the number of shops/outlets might be the most appropriate measure to use.
  - Stock market valuation and capital employed can also be used.

OCR AS Business Studies

Objectives

Any business needs to have a target that indicates what it hopes to achieve. Profitability is likely to be part of a business's objectives, but it is unlikely to be the only objective.

Why set objectives?

For a business, the advantages of setting objectives for the future are:
- They provide a sense of direction, helping employees to know what is expected of them.
- They are a source of motivation for employees, which can improve performance and efficiency.
- They help to control the operation of the business.

Mission statement

A company's mission statement sets out the purpose of the business and is published for stakeholders to see. It is a general statement lacking specific details.

Aims and goals

Aims or goals are more specific than a mission statement. They usually include:
- **Survival.** For a new business the most important aim is to survive.
- **Breaking even.** There are many costs to be covered, so a business that is surviving may then want to ensure that all its costs are covered.
- **Growth and market share.** Once a business is established, it may want to grow and capture a larger share of the market.
- **Profit.** This is a longer-term objective than survival for any business. It depends on the business's success and the level of competition it faces.

Strategic and tactical objectives

Companies try to achieve their aims by setting objectives. Objectives can be strategic or tactical.

Knowledge check 17

What is the difference between a mission statement and an objective?

Strategic objectives

- Strategic objectives are long-term objectives for the business.
- They are set by the directors or senior managers.
- They affect the business as a whole.
- They are achieved by the day-to-day use of tactical objectives.

Examples of strategic objectives are to achieve a growth rate of 10% in sales within 2 years and to diversify into new markets.

Tactical objectives

- Tactical objectives are short-term objectives for the business which are used day to day.
- They are set or implemented by middle and junior managers.
- They help in the achievement of strategic objectives.

Examples of tactical objectives are to implement a marketing strategy for a new product in order to increase sales by 10% and to introduce a new payment system for all employees so that productivity improves.

Setting objectives

The usual criterion for setting objectives is that they should be SMART. This means that they should be:

- **Specific.** Everyone should understand them.
- **Measurable.** It should be possible to quantify whether the objective has been achieved.
- **Agreed.** This makes it more likely that the objective will be achieved. Agreement should be reached by different departments and all concerned.
- **Realistic.** If an objective is unrealistic, it can result in demotivation for the workforce, who will never be able to achieve the target that has been set.
- **Time-bound.** A time limit needs to be set in which the objectives must be reached.

Constraints

It is possible that internal or external constraints will prevent an objective being achieved or slow down progress towards its achievement. Constraints can be either internal or external.

Internal constraints

These include:

- lack of finance
- poor communication
- conflict between departments
- industrial disputes

External constraints

These include:

- the state of the economy
- the behaviour of competitors
- the opinions and behaviour of external stakeholders, such as the local community

Decision making and opportunity cost

Opportunity cost is a concept that is involved in decision making. It is the value of an alternative that has to be sacrificed in order to choose another option.

Decisions involve weighing up alternatives and may require a sacrifice of one thing in order to do something else. The choice may be paying higher wages now or investing in new machinery which offers the possibility of making greater profit in the future.

Opportunity cost is particularly important for governments. A choice may have to be made between spending on the National Health Service and building a new road.

SWOT analysis

Before setting objectives, businesses often carry out a SWOT analysis to help identify successful and problem areas for the firm. SWOT stands for strengths, weaknesses, opportunities and threats (see Figure 4).

Figure 4 SWOT analysis

The strengths and weaknesses are **internal** to the business. They could be factors like a well-trained workforce or poor communications on a split site.

The opportunities and threats are **external**: for example, new markets opening up or a competitor with a popular new product.

SWOT analysis can be carried out in departments or in the firm as a whole. It is a forward-looking tool that shows the business what actions need to be taken in the future. Businesses need to change and adapt in response to the information provided by the SWOT analysis.

Social objectives

Businesses increasingly want to be seen to be caring for their employees and for the community in which they operate. They are also increasingly concerned about the effects of their business on the environment. Reduction of waste, increasing recycling and the minimisation of their carbon footprint have become increasingly important.

On occasions, social and corporate responsibility may conflict. For example, the shareholders may not be happy if a business spends too much money on 'green' activities because it may reduce the dividend they receive.

Many businesses are now very anxious to show consumers that their supplies are produced under fair trade conditions. An example is Marks and Spencer's use of 'green' cotton.

Changing objectives

The objectives of a business change over time and the business may need to alter its plans. However, only in extreme cases will a business change its strategic plans.

Examiner tip

The ability to consider the opportunity cost as well as the financial cost of a business's decision will strengthen your answer.

SWOT analysis

A technique that a business uses to consider internal (strengths and weaknesses) and external (opportunities and threats) factors. Once this has been done, objectives that are appropriate to the business's situation can be set.

Knowledge check 20

What are 'social objectives'?

For example, the banking crisis of 2008/09 forced businesses in the financial sector to adjust their plans for the future. Building societies had to make new plans for mortgage lending.

Analysis

Analysis can be achieved by examining the ways in which a business sets objectives and by looking at how this might affect its actions. For example, you could explain that setting SMART objectives would help the business to achieve a goal such as increasing profit by 5% in the next 2 years.

Evaluation

Evaluation involves coming to a conclusion about the usefulness of setting objectives. It might also involve discussion about what sort of an objective is achievable for a particular firm. There may be opportunities for evaluative comments when discussing the factors that explain why objectives change over time.

Summary

- Objectives are essential to give a business a sense of direction.
- Objectives can be long term (strategic) or short term (tactical).
- Successful objectives are likely to be SMART.
- The circumstances in which a business finds itself can affect progress towards an objective. Constraints are factors that can prevent an objective from being achieved or slow down progress towards its achievement.
- Decision making involves the concept of opportunity cost. This is not the financial cost of a decision but is what has to be forfeited when a course of action is chosen. Businesses do not have sufficient resources to do everything they would like to do and so decisions which involve an opportunity cost have to be made about priorities.
- Strategic decisions about objectives are often made following a SWOT analysis.
- Not all objectives are concerned with financial matters such as sales and profit. A business might adopt social objectives relating to stakeholders such as the local community, e.g. reducing its carbon footprint.
- A review of progress towards the achievement of objectives needs to be undertaken regularly to ensure that the business is 'on track'. If circumstances change then a business may need to adapt its objectives. An inability or refusal to do this can cause a business to fail.

Market A place where buyers and sellers meet to try to establish a price. This could be a situation like a town market where there are many buyers and sellers or it could be a situation where there is a single seller (e.g. of a house) and many buyers. Buyers and sellers do not have to meet face to face for a market to exist, e.g. eBay.

The market

Microeconomics is the study of individual consumers, businesses and markets rather than of the economy as a whole.

In economic terms, a market is a situation where buyers and sellers are brought together. It is the interaction of demand from consumers and supply from producers to establish a market **price**.

The price that a business charges is important because competitors may be charging different prices. If competitors' prices are lower, the business might have to reduce its price or take action to inform consumers that its product is better in some way. A lower price may attract more sales, but each firm needs to ensure that its price covers its costs and gives a profit.

Determination of price

Price is determined by the interaction of demand and supply.

Demand

Demand does not mean the desire to buy something. We might all want a Ferrari, but that does not mean that we will go into the market to demand one.

Demand is the quantity of a particular good that will be purchased, at a particular price, in a particular period of time. For example, it could be said that the demand for plasma screen televisions at £500 is 10,000 a week.

As a general rule, the demand for a good or service will fall as its price rises.

For some goods, demand will fall as price falls. This might be the case if consumers think that the fall in price is caused by inferior quality.

The quantity demanded at each price is known as a **demand schedule**. An example is shown in Figure 5.

Price (£)	Quantity demanded per day
20	500
25	400
30	300
35	200

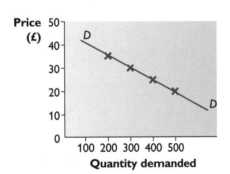

Figure 5 Demand schedule and demand curve

Figure 5 also shows the information from the demand schedule in graphical form. The price is drawn on the vertical axis and the quantity demanded on the horizontal axis. Although the line is a straight line, it is still always referred to as a **demand curve**.

Supply

Supply is the quantity offered for sale by the producer, at a given price, in a particular time period. If price rises, the producer will supply more because it can make more profit.

The quantity supplied at each price is known as a **supply schedule**. An example with its corresponding **supply curve** are given in Figure 6. Price is again on the vertical axis and, this time, quantity supplied is on the horizontal axis.

Demand and supply
Demand refers to the willingness and ability of consumers to buy a product; it is not a wish list of purchases. This is often called 'effective demand'. Similarly, supply refers to what a firm (or market) is willing and able to supply, not what it would like to supply in an ideal world.

Price (£)	Quantity demanded per day
20	100
25	200
30	300
35	400

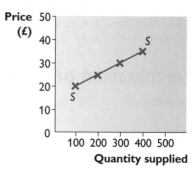

Figure 6 Supply schedule and supply curve

Equilibrium price

The equilibrium price is the price at which consumers' demand for a good or service matches the amount that suppliers put on to the market. If you look at the figures in the previous demand and supply schedules, you will see that this happens when the price is £30 and 300 units are demanded and supplied. This equilibrium is shown in Figure 7.

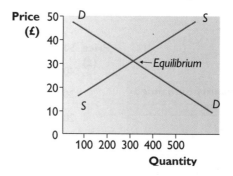

Figure 7 Equilibrium price

Equilibrium is achieved by the interaction of demand and supply through price. It is the point at which demand and supply are equal. Demand and supply do not have a direct effect on each other; however, they do affect the market price.

If more Easter eggs are produced than people will want to buy, the price of the eggs will fall. As the price of Easter eggs falls, demand for them will begin to rise, moving the market towards equilibrium (see Figure 8).

Similarly, if insufficient copies of a new game are produced, its price will rise on the market, causing firms to increase supply (see Figure 8).

For a normal good, there is always a tendency for the market to return to equilibrium as changes in price affect the quantity supplied and demanded.

Knowledge check 21

What two factors determine the market price?

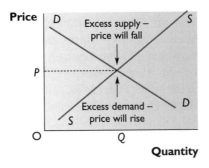

Figure 8 Achieving equilibrium

Factors that influence demand

Demand is affected by the following factors:

- **Price.** As already explained, if the price changes, the consumer moves *along* the existing demand curve. If factors other than price change (see the list below), the demand curve shifts to the right or the left, as shown in Figure 9.

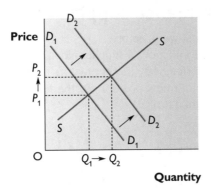

Figure 9 A rightward shift in the demand curve (increase in demand)

- **Income.** Changes in income or expectations of changes in income will affect consumer demand. It usually is the case that demand increases with income, but for some goods, such as 'value' ranges in supermarkets, demand will fall as income rises.
- **Wealth.** Wealth is a combination of savings, shares and the ownership of property. Changes in wealth or an expectation of a change in wealth will affect demand. For example, if a person expects to inherit a large amount of money, he or she may start to spend more on luxuries.
- **Advertising and promotion.** Businesses use advertising to try to increase levels of demand for their products. If demand increases, the demand curve will shift to the right.
- **Tastes and fashion.** Businesses in the clothing sector will expect demand for their products to rise and fall rapidly as the seasons change and new fashions are introduced.

- **Demographic changes.** Changes in the size or structure of the population will affect demand for different products. For example, the increasing population of elderly retired has increased demand for cruises and accompanied holidays.
- **Government action.** Government campaigns on the dangers of smoking or the benefits of eating '5 a day' can either decrease or increase the demand for products.
- **Price of a substitute.** If the price of beef rises, consumers may move to a cheaper alternative, so the demand for chicken will increase (shift to right). The demand for chicken will rise despite the fact that its price has not changed.
- **Price of a complementary good.** Complementary goods are goods that are used together. If the price of games consoles falls, the demand for them will rise, but so will the demand for games to use on the console. Their demand will rise even though their price has not changed.

Substitutes and complementary goods are important when a firm is considering price changes. A business with a product that has a large number of close substitutes will have to consider price rises very carefully. Similarly, a firm like Nintendo will need to realise that if it puts up the price of a Wii console, this will affect the demand for the whole range of products that it produces to use with the console.

Factors that influence supply

Supply is affected by the following factors:

- **Price.** A change in price will move a supplier along an existing supply curve. More will be supplied as the price rises. If other factors change (see the list below), the supply curve will shift to a new position: to the left if supply falls, as shown in Figure 10, and to the right if it rises.

Examiner tip

Think of supply and demand graphs as an easy way of demonstrating the effects of a change in the market. Drawing a graph first can clarify the effect of the change before you start to write your analysis.

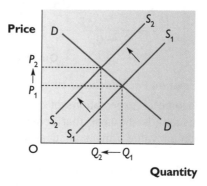

Figure 10 A leftward shift in the supply curve (decrease in supply)

- **Costs.** If any of the business's costs rise, the supply curve will shift to the left. If costs fall, the supply curve will shift to the right. These costs include raw materials, wages and salaries, and interest charges on loans.
- **Taxes.** If the government imposes a tax on a product, this will shift the supply curve to the left because it increases the firm's costs.
- **Subsidies.** If the government wants to encourage the supply of a product such as organic food, it might give a subsidy. This will shift the supply curve to the right.

- **Price of other products.** This is known as **competitive supply**. Suppose a business supplies a range of soft drinks. A fall in the price of one drink will make it more profitable for the firm to supply more of the other drinks in its range.
- **Weather.** The supply of agricultural products is likely to be greatly affected by the weather. Droughts or excessive rainfall will affect crop yields and, therefore, the amount coming to market.

Interaction of demand and supply

It is now possible to see how demand and supply interact with each other through changes in price.

Change in demand

In Figure 11, there is an increase in the demand for fresh fruit because of a government healthy eating campaign. The initial equilibrium is at a price P_1 and the quantity is Q_1. The rise in demand following the government campaign will shift the demand curve to the right. The new equilibrium leads to more being demanded and supplied (Q_2) at a higher price (P_2).

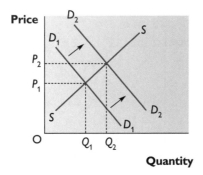

Figure 11 Effect of an increase in demand on equilibrium price and quantity

Figure 12 shows the opposite situation, where there is a fall in demand. The outbreak of bird flu at Bernard Matthews' turkey farms is an example. The effect was to move the demand curve to the left, with less being demanded and supplied at a lower price.

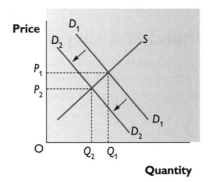

Figure 12 Effect of a decrease in demand on equilibrium price and quantity

Examiner tip

A knowledge of the factors affecting supply and demand can be useful in producing an analytical answer. For example, if a 'green tax' is put on the output of a firm that pollutes the environment this means that either the firm will have a lower profit or it must find some way to lower costs if it wants to keep profit at the same level.

Change in supply

In the next two examples, it is the supply curve that shifts.

Suppose that the price of potatoes falls rapidly because of a good harvest. This means that crisp manufacturers have to pay less for raw materials. As a result of this they will increase supply, moving the supply curve to the right. More will be supplied at a lower price, as shown in Figure 13.

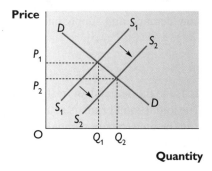

Figure 13 Effect of an increase in supply on equilibrium price and quantity

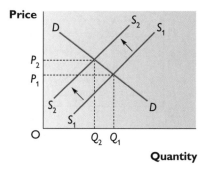

Figure 14 Effect of a decrease in supply on equilibrium price and quantity

If the price of oil rises on international markets, the plastics industry will face higher costs because oil is one of its main costs of production. The supply curve will shift to the left, resulting in less being supplied at a higher price, as shown in Figure 14.

Elasticity of demand and supply

- **Price elasticity** of demand shows how responsive demand is to a change in price.
- Price elasticity of supply shows how responsive supply is to a change in price.
- If demand and supply are not responsive to a change in price, they are said to be inelastic.

Elasticity of demand

Goods with elastic demand tend to have the following characteristics:
- They are luxuries, rather than necessities.
- Substitutes are readily available.
- They take a relatively large proportion of consumers' income.

Price elasticity This shows how responsive demand and supply are to a price change. If demand and supply are elastic, a small change in price brings a proportionately larger change in the quantities demanded and supplied, e.g. a 5% fall in price brings about a 15% increase in demand. If demand and supply are inelastic a change in price brings a proportionately smaller change in the quantities demanded and supplied, e.g. a 5% rise in price only brings a 2% increase in the quantity supplied.

If the demand curve is inelastic, it will be quite steep. For inelastic demand, a small fall in price will have an even smaller effect on the quantity demanded.

A product like local bus travel will have inelastic demand. If the price goes down, it will not attract a large proportion of new customers. Those who need to use the bus will have to continue doing so; those who have cars or who walk are unlikely to be affected by the price fall.

If the demand curve is elastic, it will be quite flat. For elastic demand, a small fall in price will have a larger effect on demand.

A product like a plasma television is likely to have elastic demand. As its price falls, it will attract a larger proportion of new buyers than the percentage fall in price.

It is important for a firm to know whether the demand for its product is elastic or inelastic when it comes to changing price. Firms facing inelastic demand will know that they can put price up without having much effect on demand; those facing elastic demand will have to think carefully before raising prices.

Elasticity of supply

When supply is elastic, the supply curve will be quite flat. For elastic supply, a small fall in price will lead to a large change in the quantity supplied.

When supply is inelastic, the supply curve will be steeper. For inelastic supply, a small change in price will have little effect on supply.

Goods with inelastic supply will be produced in a situation where it is not possible to respond quickly to changes in price. This may be because labour or raw materials are not available or because production takes a long time. Examples of goods with inelastic supply are ships, oil, metals and agricultural products like apples.

Examiner tip
Knowledge of elasticity can help strengthen your analysis of a change in the market, e.g. the demand for petrol is highly inelastic and so a rise in price will only have a small effect on demand. Assuming that costs stay the same this means that the profit levels of petrol companies will rise.

Classification of markets and types of competition

Competitive markets

In competitive markets:
- There are a large number of firms in the market.
- Businesses find it difficult to change price. If they do raise price, consumers may switch to a competitor.
- Prices are kept down, which is good for consumers.
- Innovation is encouraged.

Monopoly

A monopoly is a market controlled by one firm. Monopolies have the following characteristics:
- The monopolist can control the market because it is the only supplier of the product.
- The monopolist can charge any price.
- Monopoly is most common among utility suppliers, such as the water companies.

- Monopolists may not act in the interests of consumers, although this is not always the case.
- In UK law, a monopolist controls at least 25% of the market.
- Monopolists may have the power to drive other firms out of business.

Oligopoly

An oligopoly is a market dominated by a few large firms, such as petrol supply. In an oligopoly situation:

- There may be other smaller firms in the market.
- The firms are very concerned about their share of the total market (e.g. supermarkets).
- If one firm cuts prices, the others are likely to follow. This can start a price war.
- If one firm raises prices, the others are likely to hold back for as long as possible to try to earn more revenue and gain market share.
- It is possible for oligopolists to **collude** (agree to set prices), although this is illegal.

Opportunities for analysis

Changes of price and their effect on the market give numerous opportunities for analysis. For example, you might say: If the business raises the price of its product, it may find that its sales fall dramatically. The product has been shown to have high price elasticity of demand and the price rise will, therefore, lead to a larger than proportionate fall in demand and a fall in revenue.

Alternatively: This firm is in an oligopolistic market facing fierce competition from a few competitors. If the firm raises prices, it may find that its competitors do not follow. This will mean a loss of revenue and market share in the short run.

Evaluation

For evaluation, it might be possible to make recommendations on price changes for a business, depending on the type of elasticity it faces or the type of market in which it operates.

Summary

- Market price is determined by supply from producers and demand from consumers.
- Factors affecting demand include price, income, wealth, advertising/promotion, tastes and fashion, prices of substitutes and complements.
- Factors affecting supply include price, taxes on the product, subsidies, and costs of production.
- Price is important to a firm because if its price is out of line with the ruling price in the market, demand for its products will fall. Price also affects the firm's mark up.
- Price elasticity measures the way in which supply and demand for a product react when market price changes.
- Demand will be inelastic where there are few substitutes for a product. Thus a firm can try to raise prices because it is likely that demand will not fall by much. With many substitutes this will not be possible and demand will be elastic.
- Supply will be inelastic if it is not easy to expand production. If it is easy and/or the firm is holding large stocks then supply will be elastic.

Other influences

Technology

In recent times, it has become increasingly important for businesses to keep up with changes in technology. The technological changes might be in the production process, giving improvements in productivity and efficiency, or they might mean that the business needs to update its product.

Examples of technological progress

Some examples of technological progress which have enabled improvements in productivity and efficiency in each of the three main business sectors of the economy are given below.

Primary sector

- Increased mechanisation in farming.
- Extraction of oil and ores using new equipment.
- Improvements in crops to make them more resistant to disease.

Secondary sector

- Computer-aided design.
- Safety technology applied to products like cars.
- Development of information technology (IT), the internet and communications.
- Control over production/quality using computers.

Tertiary sector

- Point-of-sale equipment in shops to improve stock control and distribution.
- Internet selling.
- Electronic transfer of information.
- Video conferencing.
- Home working.

Opportunities and threats

Opportunities from new technology

Technological progress offers opportunities for:
- greater efficiency
- reduced costs
- better quality control
- shorter lead times

Threats from new technology

However, new technology also poses several problems:
- the need for expensive and time-consuming research to keep up to date
- the threat to jobs

Productivity A measure of the efficiency of a firm's production process. Assume that 10 employees produce 100 units in an hour. If new capital equipment is installed and now 5 employees produce 100 units in an hour, those employees have become twice as productive and the firm is more efficient. Technology is a key driving force in improving productivity and efficiency.

Knowledge check 23

What is meant by the terms 'productivity' and 'efficiency'?

Demography The study of demographics includes research into changes in the population's age, gender, and ethnic origin. Businesses use demographic data to make decisions about who to target their products at and how best to do this.

- the need for employees to retrain to use the new technology
- difficult decisions about when to invest in new technology

Analysis

Analysis can be achieved in discussions about technology by looking at the costs involved in keeping up to date with changes and the impact of this on the profits of the business.

Evaluation

Evaluation could be achieved by weighing up short-term costs against long-term gains in sales/market share/profit. Alternatively, it is possible to weigh up which changes in technology are likely to have the biggest impact on the business in the future.

Social demographics

Demography is the study of population structure. The distribution of population and changes in its distribution are vitally important external factors that influence demand for the goods and services that businesses supply.

Size and structure of the UK population

- The UK population is rising. In 2008, it was around 60 million.
- The percentage of older people in the population is growing annually. (The UK has an **ageing population**.)
- The number of younger people is falling.
- The EU population is ageing more rapidly than that of the UK.

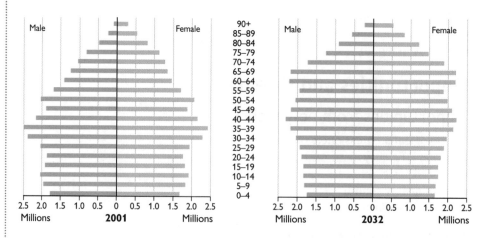

Source: Government Actuary's Department

Figure 15 UK population by age and sex, 2001 and 2032 (projected)

Source: Government Actuary's Department

The reasons for these changes in the size and distribution of the UK population are:
- an increase in the birth rate
- a fall in the death rate
- more people settling in the UK than leaving it

Implications of social demographics for business

Effects of changing demand

- More goods and services are needed for the elderly, such as care homes, escorted holidays and stair lifts. This is referred to as a growth in the 'grey economy'.
- The demand for public sector services is changing. More doctors, hospital beds and day centres are needed, but fewer school places, as death rates fall and birth rate growth slows.
- The tax burden on those in work is increasing because those in work have to pay for public services to be provided by government.
- As people live longer, the pressure on both public and private pensions is increasing. In addition, many private pension funds are struggling to pay pensions because of falling contributions as a result of fewer workers contributing to the fund. The government is facing similar difficulties with the state pension.
- There have also been changes in the ethnic mix in the UK. This is leading to changes in goods and services demanded and supplied (e.g. there is increased demand for a range of ethnic foods in supermarkets).

Changing employment patterns

- A smaller proportion of young workers will lead to skill shortages as older workers retire.
- There is an increasing need for training and apprenticeships to equip workers with skills for the future.
- There is an increasing use of retired workers in some sectors. For example, B&Q finds retired workers more reliable and less likely to be absent than some younger employees.

Analysis

Marks for analysis could be gained by explaining the reaction of businesses to changes in the distribution of population and in the resultant demand for their products. For example, a holiday company like Thomas Cook may decide that it needs to begin to offer more cruises to meet the growing demand among the newly retired who have money to spend. If they are successful in generating more demand for these cruises, the revenue and profit they earn will rise.

Evaluation

This could be achieved by discussing the need for Thomas Cook to spend money in the short run in setting up these cruises, with the likelihood of achieving higher profit in the long run as demand for its holidays rises.

Knowledge check 24

Give three reasons why a business needs to take account of changing demographic factors.

Examiner tip

Although you will not be expected to know actual figures for population change, it would be useful to have some idea of the changes taking place. This allows you to show your knowledge. For example, the fact that there is a smaller proportion of younger people will create a skill shortage as older people retire. Employers will then need to consider employing older or retired workers, as B&Q has done.

Ethics and corporate social responsibility

What is meant by ethical behaviour?

- **Ethical behaviour** means doing the right thing.
- It involves a moral code of conduct.
- It can be a matter of opinion.
- Unethical behaviour is not the same thing as illegal behaviour.

Unethical behaviour by a business

Examples of a business behaving unethically (but not necessarily illegally) are:
- paying only the minimum wage
- providing only basic health and safety training for employees
- paying high rates of pay to senior managers while freezing other employees' pay
- delaying paying suppliers for as long as possible
- not publishing full accounting information with the intention of misleading
- dealing with countries with poor human rights
- importing from countries where labour is exploited

Unethical behaviour by employees

Examples of unethical behaviour by employees are:
- overstating expenses
- using business equipment such as stationery and telephones for personal use
- taking time off by pretending to be ill

Benefits of a business behaving ethically

Towards employees

- Ethical treatment of employees improves motivation and therefore may improve productivity and profitability for the firm.
- Ethical firms might be more attractive to new recruits and consequently attract the highest-quality labour when taking on new staff.
- Concern about green issues among young people — particularly graduates — means that businesses trying to protect the environment are more likely to encourage well-qualified applicants.

Towards suppliers

- It builds a good relationship with suppliers if payments are made promptly.
- Suppliers might be more ready to respond to an emergency or last-minute order.

Towards the local community

- Ethical behaviour gives the business a good reputation among local people, which generates good local publicity.
- Sales in the local area are likely to improve.

Other benefits

- Ethical behaviour generates good advertising and publicity for the business.
- It sets an example to others.
- If the firm is recognised by government, the financial sector and the media as an ethical business, this may encourage investment in the future.
- Ethical behaviour can be used as a marketing strategy.

Costs of an ethical approach

- Are stakeholders happy with the costs this approach imposes on the business?
- An ethical approach takes time for directors and employees to implement.
- Employees may need training.
- Sourcing ethical suppliers may be expensive.
- Share prices may fall because the business's funds are now being used differently.

Corporate social responsibility

Corporate social responsibility (CSR) is known as the stakeholder approach. It involves:

- purchasing materials from sustainable sources
- trying to minimise the effects of redundancies
- minimising environmental damage
- insisting on using ethical suppliers

Problems with the stakeholder approach

- Businesses need to balance the needs of different stakeholders, such as shareholders and employees. Employees might feel that a profit-sharing scheme would be an attractive idea, but the shareholders might be resistant because it could reduce their dividends.
- Are the shareholders more important because of their input of capital and their power to vote at the AGM?
- There will always be losers as well as winners in any decision implemented by a business. The managers need to ensure that they do all they can to keep every stakeholder happy, if possible.
- Is CSR simply a marketing tool to try to win business?

Analysis

Analysis marks in this area can be achieved by discussing the impact of deciding whether or not to implement new technology. If the firm chooses to use new technology, this will have cost implications through the investment required in new equipment and also because of the need to train staff in using the new machines. If a firm chooses not to implement new technology, the result may be a loss of sales and market share, which is likely to result in lower turnover for the business.

> **Examiner tip**
> It is important to recognise and be able to analyse the costs as well as the benefits to a business of adopting an ethical approach. For example, sourcing from small producers locally could mean losing the bulk discounts available from larger (but less ethical) national suppliers.

> **Corporate social responsibility** The process whereby a business monitors and ensures its compliance not only with the law but with accepted ethical standards as well. It has to be a genuine objective which permeates the entire firm if it is to succeed.

Evaluation

The easiest way to gain evaluation marks when discussing new technology is to compare the short-term cost of the investment with the long-term gains to be made in terms of sales, turnover and profit from being at the forefront of the market. It is also possible to compare the high risk of being one of the first to take on new technology with the risk of it failing. An alternative way to achieve evaluation marks is to highlight which ethical act is the most significant to the business in this context. It is also possible to look at which action will be easiest or cheapest to undertake.

Summary

- Technology takes many forms. Basically, it is any innovation that allows a business to become more productive and therefore produce in a more efficient manner.

- Technology affects businesses in all three sectors of the economy: primary, secondary and tertiary.

- Technology brings opportunities (e.g. the possibility of lower unit costs) but also threats (e.g. the loss of jobs and therefore employee unrest).

- It is likely that new technology, whatever form it takes, will affect several, or all, departments of a firm: finance, production, human resources and marketing.

- Ethical behaviour is not absolute in the way that laws are. This means that 'acting unethically' is not the same as 'acting illegally'.

- What is considered as ethical behaviour will differ from business to business and from person to person.

- There are costs as well as benefits to a business in acting in an ethical manner.

- Corporate social responsibility (CSR) has to be a serious initiative that runs throughout the whole business if it is to succeed.

- CSR and an ethical approach will not guarantee that all stakeholders in a business are always satisfied; some stakeholders may lose out in the short term.

OCR AS Business Studies

How to use this section

This section comprises two case studies. Both have been written to reflect accurately the type of questions you will face in your examination for Unit F291. The format and the mark allocation mirror what you will be faced with in the unit examination.

It is strongly recommended that you attempt the questions before you read the examiner's comments and the student answers. This will encourage you to practise your exam technique and allow you to compare your answers with those provided. Once you have attempted the case study questions, it is recommended that you look at the initial examiner's comments, which highlight the type of answer expected by the examiner (shown by the icon ⓔ).

Following this are answers written by students. Included within these answers are letters **a**, **b** etc. which correspond to examiner's comments on each answer. These comments are intended to show you exactly what is rewarded and what is not. They also clearly highlight within the student answers where a particular level of response is achieved. These examiner's comments are preceded by the icon ⓔ.

At the beginning of the examiner's comments, the mark awarded for the question is shown. A total mark is then shown, together with the grade awarded, at the end of each set of answers. All answers are A grades.

Levels of response

One of the key routes to success is understanding levels of response. Answering the questions using the appropriate level of response will mean that you are approaching the question in the right manner. Understanding how examiners use 'trigger words' will help you to identify which level of response is required.

Level of response	Definition
Level 1	**Knowledge** • Business knowledge or facts
Level 2	**Explanation or application** • An explanation or understanding of knowledge
Level 3	**Analysis** • Implications for the business • How the business is affected • The reaction of a business or stakeholder • All should be in the context of the case.
Level 4	**Evaluation** • Making a justified judgement in the context of the case • Weighing the evidence/argument/long term and short term in the context of the case • Suggesting which issue raised is the most significant, the most likely to affect the business or the most serious factor to affect the business

Mastering what is required for each level of response should be a high priority.

Ensuring that you are able to offer analysis and evaluation is essential if you are to achieve the top grades.

Analysis

Consider the example of Business A which is about to invest in new technology by buying a new machine. The following paragraphs show how easy it is to gain a Level 3 (L3) mark.

The owners of the business will be able to produce more items as the new machine is much more efficient. Therefore with more goods being produced, the business will be able to increase its revenue from the extra sales. This additional revenue will help the business to make more profit (L3) and therefore it will be able to offer a higher dividend to its shareholders (L3).

Being able to produce more goods with the new machine may, however, lead to a fall in the number of employees who are needed. The employees may therefore either lose their jobs or be fearful of losing their jobs, which may affect their productivity (L3).

With the new machine and the subsequent increase in output, the suppliers to the business will have the opportunity to sell more of their components and therefore increase their sales revenue. It may mean the supplier will need to take on more employees (L3), which will benefit the government, as it will have to pay out less in job seeker's allowance (L3).

Clearly stating the likely implications for the business or stakeholders, or how the business may react, in the context of the case is a common and effective way in which you can gain Level 3 marks.

Evaluation

Similarly, evaluative statements require you to make a justified judgement. The judgement can be related to the most likely effect, or the factor that will have the most beneficial or detrimental effect upon the business. The following paragraph shows you how to achieve Level 4 (L4) by using evaluation.

The stakeholder which will benefit the most is likely to be the shareholder. As a result of the increased output from the new machine, it is very likely that the increased sales will mean additional profits that could be distributed in the form of dividends to the shareholders. This is more certain than the possibility of redundancies as a result of the machine. It is not certain if the machine is used instead of employees. With the increased output the firm may actually require additional employees and not fewer (L4).

Here the student has made a judgement which suggests that one group of stakeholders will benefit more than another and has justified this view in the context of the case.

It is not enough just to begin your answer 'In evaluation' — you have to make an actual judgement that has been justified in context.

Trigger words

Each question will have a key trigger word or phrase that should give you a clear indication of the appropriate level of response. These are listed in the following table. Levels of response are also referred to as assessment objectives (AOs).

Trigger words	Level of response	Assessment objective
State, list	Level 1	AO1
Explain, outline, describe	Level 2	AO2
Analyse	Level 3	AO3
Evaluate, assess, to what extent, discuss, recommend	Level 4	AO4

Mark allocation

	Mark allocation
6-mark question	• Level 3, 5–6 marks • Level 2, 3–4 marks • Level 1, 1–2 marks
10-mark question	• Level 3, 7–10 marks • Level 2, 3–6 marks • Level 1, 1–2 marks
14-mark question	• Level 4, 11–14 marks • Level 3, 7–10 marks • Level 2, 4–6 marks • Level 1, 1–3 marks
18-mark question	• Level 4, 14–18 marks • Level 3, 9–13 marks • Level 2, 5–8 marks • Level 1, 1–4 marks

Examination format

It is important that you are aware of the examination format. Your teacher will no doubt have made this clear to you at an early stage in the course, but the format is summarised here.

- Length of examination: 1 hour.
- The total marks for this paper represent 40% of the total AS marks.

This is an unseen data–response paper, where the stimulus material is approximately 300 words in length.

There are five questions which can come from any section of the specification. There are usually two questions that have more than one part to them: for example, (a) and (b). The questions will be a combination of short-answer, 'state'-type questions, 'analyse' questions and two questions that will require you to evaluate.

You will have to answer the questions in an answer booklet. This contains each question followed by a space for your answer.

Weightings for the different assessment objectives (levels of response) as a percentage of the total AS marks are shown in the table below.

	AO1 (L1)	AO2 (L2)	AO3 (L3)	AO4 (L4)	Total
An Introduction to Business	14%	10%	10%	6%	40%

Case studies

The examination papers you take at AS and A2 are based on case studies, so it is essential that you are able to use the context of the case. In order to do this, it is worthwhile adopting the 'first read' and 'second read' approach.

First read

Read the case quickly to ascertain:

- the type of business (its legal status — Ltd, plc, sole trader) or its age or size
- the product or service
- the consumers
- the objectives of the business

These four factors will provide you with a framework in which to answer the questions.

Second read

Read the questions and then read the case again. This is a more thorough read when you can start looking for information within the case to answer the questions posed.

For Unit F291, although the case material is only approximately 300 words, it still provides a context. For Level 3 and Level 4 answers, you are expected to use the context in order to gain the marks.

Case study 1 **Warburtons**

1 hour

Warburtons, the privately owned family baker, is now the UK's second biggest food brand after Coca-Cola. In recent years the business has built new bakeries and extensions to its existing plants in Scotland and Yorkshire. In its Yorkshire bakery, Warburtons can produce 2 million loaves of bread and 500,000 bread rolls a week. In addition the company has branched out from its traditional markets in the north of the UK by building a bakery in London. In investing in all this expansion, the Warburtons management is gambling on the continued growth of the bread market in the UK.

At the same time, Warburtons has seen an increased willingness among UK consumers to try different types of bread, other than the traditional sliced loaves and bread rolls. There has been a big increase in recent years in the demand for speciality breads offered by the major supermarkets and smaller craft bakeries. The profits to be made in this area of the market are usually much bigger than those for traditional bread. Warburtons does not produce own-label bread for any of the major supermarkets and it is in this area that it now faces its main competition.

More recently, Warburtons has been in the press because of the high salt content of its bread. Under pressure from the Government's Food Standards Agency, manufacturers have been asked to reduce salt levels in all processed foods. Some have acted more quickly than others. The press revealed that some Warburtons loaves contain half a gram of salt, meaning that a 5-year-old would reach a safe salt intake limit after eating three sandwiches. Bread is the main source of salt in the UK diet and 3 million people eat Warburtons' bread every day. In response Warburtons says that it is aiming to meet the government target by 2010.

By 2011, Warburtons had reduced the salt content of its bread from 700 mg per 100 g of bread to 430 mg. This was achieved at a considerable cost to the company in terms of research and development without compromising the taste of the bread for the consumer.

In the same year, Warburtons introduced a gluten-free range of bread and in June 2011, it added to its product range with rolls and baps for BBQ eating.

Questions

(1) Warburtons uses a range of machines to produce its bread. The machines are an example of a factor of production — capital. State three other factors of production. (3 marks)

ⓔ This is a 'state' question and therefore it is only necessary to state or list the other factors of production. The examiner is looking for land, labour and enterprise.

(2) (a) Analyse one reason why Warburtons may undertake market research. (6 marks)

ⓔ The trigger word for this question is 'analyse' so a Level 3 response is required. Highlighting how Warburtons may need market research and how it would benefit is one route to a Level 3 answer. The implication of undertaking such research in terms of costs is another possible route. However, it is essential that you refer directly to Warburtons in order to avoid a generic answer.

Warburtons has already noticed that consumers are willing to try a wider range of types of bread. Consequently, further research would allow Warburtons to satisfy the recent trends in tastes of its consumers. It could also undertake research in order to find out how important the level of salt content is to the consumer. It may want to undertake more research into its new market in London, as tastes in this area are likely to be different from those of its traditional market.

The question asks you to analyse only *one* reason so you should tackle only one. There are no additional marks for those who offer two reasons.

(2) (b) Other than market research, evaluate the factors that will affect the success of Warburtons. (14 marks)

@ There are several key words in this question. 'Other than' requires you to consider anything apart from market research. There are no marks for making comments related to market research, which will waste valuable time. 'Evaluate' indicates that a Level 4 answer is required and that you will need to offer a justified judgement.

You also need to think about the criteria for 'success' and ensure you are considering success for Warburtons. The extent to which it is achieving its objectives is one measure of success. Achieving high levels of profit, satisfying its stakeholders, meeting targets and ensuring the new bakery in London is established are obvious objectives.

Whichever factors you consider, both internal and external, it is essential that they are related to Warburtons to ensure there is sufficient context. Note also that the question refers to 'factors' and therefore it is necessary for you to comment on at least two.

(3) State three examples of how the government could affect the operations of Warburtons. (3 marks)

@ This is another 'state' question and therefore only requires a list without explanation. The following can be used:

- government legislation (e.g. health and safety)
- taxation
- state of the economy (inflation, unemployment)

The question asks you to state how the government affects the operations of Warburtons so your answer must relate directly to the government.

(4) Analyse two reasons why the objectives of Warburtons may change. (10 marks)

@ 'Analyse' is a key word, as is 'two'. Ensuring that you analyse two reasons why the objectives of Warburtons could change is vital if you are to access all the available marks. It is also important to ensure that you refer to the objectives of Warburtons and not objectives in general.

(5) (a) Outline two ways in which technology could benefit Warburtons.   (4 marks)

ⓔ 'Outline' is a Level 2 trigger word. You will need to offer a brief explanation of how technology will benefit Warburtons specifically. The technology does not have to be complicated; you are not expected to have a working knowledge of the bakery. It is sufficient to refer to machines that help with quality or computerisation for ordering stock, or simply new technology in terms of a new oven. The key is to outline briefly a clear link between the technology and a benefit for Warburtons.

(5) (b) State two ways in which the size of Warburtons could be measured.   (2 marks)

ⓔ The trigger word is 'state' so you must just list. The size of Warburtons could be measured in many ways: the number of employees, sales or sales revenue, profits, size of plant, value of assets and number of plants (bakeries).

(5) (c) Evaluate whether the stakeholders of Warburtons will benefit from its new bakery in London.   (18 marks)

ⓔ The trigger word is 'evaluate'. Offering a justified judgement is essential for higher marks. You need to refer to more than one stakeholder and show how the stakeholders will benefit from the new bakery in London. The context of this question is very important. It is easy to talk about stakeholders, but care must be taken to ensure that the stakeholders are appropriate and that they are stakeholders of Warburtons.

Total: 60 marks

Student A

(1) Enterprise
      Land
      Labour

ⓔ **3/3 marks awarded.** The student has done exactly what is necessary and just listed the correct answers.

(2) (a) Market research is a method of finding out what the consumer wants, **a** using for example a questionnaire. This could help Warburtons to find out demand for a certain product, new or old, therefore allowing them to produce only what the consumer wants **b** and therefore enabling them to sell more of that certain product as it caters for consumer needs, so revenue will increase which therefore is return on the initial money they invested on market research. **c**

ⓔ **6/6 marks awarded.**   **a** The student has stated what market research is (Level 1). **b** Explanation is offered (Level 2). **c** The last section is clearly analysis (Level 3). There is an indication of the implications for Warburtons of undertaking the market research.

(2) (b) Competition will affect the success of Warburtons **a** because this will mean there are more competitors and this will cause consumers to buy other branded bread. **b** This may result in lower revenue for Warburtons due to competitors setting lower prices, so this will affect the success of Warburtons. **c**

Another factor that will affect the success of Warburtons is the government's Food Standards Agency releasing health warnings such as 'too much salt content in Warburtons bread'. **d** This will therefore influence the consumers to purchase less, so this will affect the success of Warburtons bread negatively because less total revenue will be made and therefore less profits. **e** So Warburtons will be less able to expand the company due to less revenue to invest.

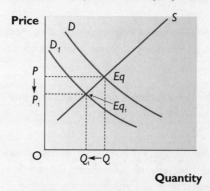

The graph shows that high salt content will therefore cause demand to decrease to D_1 (move left). Equilibrium will also decrease to Eq_1 and quantity demanded/supplied will also decrease from Q to Q_1 leading the price to decrease from P to P_1 due to the pressure from the Government's Food Standards Agency. **f**

Another factor that will affect the success of Warburtons is a decrease in number of competitors. This is beneficial because if there are less competitors this will mean that Warburtons can increase the prices of bread and consumers will still have to spend due to the bread being an inelastic good (necessity). Therefore Warburtons will make higher total revenue and higher profits so it would have extra revenue to invest into expanding. **g,h**

ⓔ 10/14 marks awarded. a Knowledge of a factor that will affect the success of Warburtons (Level 1). **b** An explanation of the factor gains a Level 2. **c** Although the student has indicated that competition will lead to lower revenue, there is no real attempt to show how that will actually affect the success of Warburtons. The student will therefore not gain a Level 3 mark at this stage. **d** Another valid factor that could affect the success of the business (Level 1). **e** This is a good example of analysis. The student has clearly shown the link between the factor (FSA) and the consequences for the business in terms of its success. **f** This is an alternative method of gaining marks for analysis. Drawing an appropriate demand and supply diagram and highlighting the key changes correctly will show the consequences for the business. **g** Using the opposite of a factor that you have already used is not always a good tactic. Unless the question has asked you to consider both options, there is no need to spell out the opposite effect. What is said would, however, be a Level 3 response in isolation. **h** Unfortunately, the student has not offered any evaluation. If he or she had gone on to suggest which of the factors would have the most significant effect on the success of the business, more marks would have been gained.

(3) Taxation
Laws
Government bodies (Food Standards Agency)

🄔 **3/3 marks awarded.** The student has correctly stated three examples of how the government affects the operations of Warburtons.

(4) The objectives of Warburtons may change for a few reasons. The economy that Warburtons is operating in may face a recession. **a** This will therefore cause consumers to spend less or purchase less. So this will mean less bread made by Warburtons will sell, therefore less profit will be made causing objectives to change. **b** Objectives such as diversify/expand may change to just making a profit. **c** Therefore a recession would cause Warburtons to change its objectives.

Another reason why Warburtons' objectives may change is a change in price of raw materials. For example, ingredients for bread may decrease in price, **d** therefore allowing Warburtons to produce at a lower cost and therefore make higher profits. This will therefore mean that objectives such as expanding and diversifying are more able to be afforded. **e** This means that Warburtons can afford to change its objectives as more profits make them more likely to be achievable (SMART). **f**

🄔 **8/10 marks awarded. a** The student has stated a reason why objectives may change (Level 1). **b** The student starts to offer a good explanation of why objectives may change. Level 2 is obvious, but Level 3 requires a clear link between the reason for change and the resulting likely change. No change is offered at this stage of the answer. **c** Although changes in the objectives are now offered, there is no real explanation or link as to why they will change. This will not gain a Level 3 mark. **d** A clear explanation of another reason for changes in objectives (Level 2). **e** The student has now made the link between the reason for change and the actual change, and consequently will be awarded a Level 3 mark. **f** This adds little to the answer. Just mentioning SMART will not necessarily mean additional marks, especially if it is not related to the question.

The question asks for two reasons why objectives may change. This student has attempted to write about two but will only be given Level 3 marks for one of the reasons. Full marks cannot be gained, even though it is still a good answer.

(5) (a) To increase production; technology can be used to make bread more quickly, therefore more can be produced in the same amount of time, therefore unit costs are reduced, allowing Warburtons to make more profit. **a**

An improvement in quality as machinery is more precise and accurate, and therefore is more likely to lead to better products and therefore higher customer satisfaction. **b**

🄔 **4/4 marks awarded. a** This is a clear outline of how technology could benefit Warburtons and would be awarded Level 2. **b** Again, the student has outlined clearly and therefore would gain a second Level 2 mark. This is the obvious link between the technology offering quality and how the quality will benefit the business by increasing customer satisfaction.

Notice that there is no need to write at length to gain both Level 2 marks. Time saved on these questions can be used effectively on the higher-mark questions.

(5) (b) Size can be measured by number of employees, number of customers and amount of bread sold.

ⓔ **2/2 marks awarded.** The student has correctly stated ways to measure the size of Warburtons. Three ways have been offered, but the first two are correct so the third is not necessary.

(5) (c) As Warburtons has chosen to open a new bakery in London, expanding its customer base, this is beneficial to employees as new labour will have to be recruited. This means an increase in income and therefore spending **a** and a reduction in unemployment in that area, therefore employees are benefited. **b** Also, other local companies in the area will benefit from the new revenue in the area, therefore leading to increased expenditure and an increase in sales for those other companies. **c**

The government will also benefit because it will no longer pay out benefits to the unemployed and can therefore spend the money on other important areas such as the health service. **d** The government might also gain more revenue from increased taxes as employees are now earning more than when unemployed. This will mean the government has more to spend on the services it provides. **e**

The suppliers of Warburtons will benefit because the new factory will require supplies of flour and other ingredients. These companies may be able to expand themselves as they will be making more profits because they can order more ingredients at a lower unit price. **f**

The one group of stakeholders to benefit the most are the additional employees. It is better to be working than at home and the new factory will have to have the new labour. But the other stakeholders may not benefit as much because we cannot be sure that employees will spend their money in other local shops. **g**

ⓔ **16/18 marks awarded. a** An appropriate stakeholder is mentioned, but although an attempt is made to offer analysis, it could be made slightly clearer who will be doing the additional spending. Level 2 marks will definitely be awarded, but a Level 3 mark is in doubt as a result of the final part of the sentence, which confuses the issue. **b** This last part of the sentence is confusingly written. It is a good illustration of why it is important to read through your answer if you have time. **c** Mentioning the increase in sales for other companies is worthy of a Level 2 mark. However, the student could have offered slightly more detail by stating how the increased sales could benefit the other companies. **d** Although put simply, this is an effective statement and would be awarded Level 3 marks. A clear benefit to the government is given, and a suggestion of how the reduction in benefit payouts could be used. **e** This is another effective statement of how the government will benefit. An additional comment concerning what it could spend the extra revenue on would have enhanced the answer still further. Nevertheless, a Level 3 would be awarded. **f** This is another effective, well-linked statement which offers clear analysis. **g** The student has clearly attempted to justify which stakeholder will benefit the most and therefore would be awarded a Level 4 mark.

ⓔ **Total: 52/60 marks — an impressive A grade.**

Student B

(1) Labour
Land
Capital

e **3/3 marks awarded.** The student has done as asked and simply stated three other factors of production. It is not necessary to waste time by adding any more detail.

(2) (a) Warburtons might use market research to find out what their customers think about their products. **a** This might tell them that customers wanted a different range of products or that they were happy with what was being produced already by Warburtons. **b** As a result of the research Warburtons could introduce new products that matched the customer demand and increase their turnover in the future. **c**

e **6/6 marks awarded.** This question asks for analysis so it is important to give the reactions of Warburtons to the market research results. **a** The answer starts off with a Level 1 statement about why the market research might have been undertaken. **b** It then goes on to discuss what Warburtons might find out from the results of the market research, which would achieve Level 2. **c** In the last sentence, the answer explains how Warburtons' response to the market research will have an effect on the financial future of the business. This is analysis in context, giving a chain from action to results, and it would achieve Level 3.

(2) (b) Other factors could also influence the success of Warburtons. Bread is a staple food with low elasticity of demand, meaning that people will continue to buy it even when their income falls. **a** Warburtons is less likely to be influenced by changes in the economy than firms producing luxury foods. However, if the population of the UK becomes more wealthy and living standards rise, Warburtons may find that people are eating less bread and substituting it with luxury products or buying specialist bread produced by craft bakeries. This might mean that their profits fall as a result. **b**

Warburtons' success may also be affected by health warnings about people eating too much bread or advice about the health benefits of eating bread. This could have an effect on the demand for their products. **c**

Warburtons also need to ensure that their products change with consumer demand. If the demand for sliced bread begins to fall, Warburtons must ensure that their product range reflects this. If they do not do this they will find the demand for their products falling and their profits might decline. **d**

I think that the most important factor that will affect Warburtons' success is the affluence of UK citizens. This is because they will probably feel the effects of improved living standards in falling sales for bread as demand for other foods increases. They may have to change their product base as a result of this if they are to maintain their sales and profit levels in the future. **e**

ⓔ **11/14 marks awarded.** This question asks for evaluation, so a Level 4 response is required. It is also important to note that the question says 'other than market research'. Any answer or part of an answer using further elements of market research will not, therefore, gain marks. **a** The student starts off by considering how the economy will affect the demand for bread and, therefore, Warburtons' success. **b** The student achieves Level 3 by going on to analyse the effect of changes in the economy and the income of consumers by considering the effect on Warburtons' profits. The statement about elasticity shows that the student understands this concept and can apply it correctly to a product like bread. Further comments at this point about the possibility of Warburtons switching to other products, like cakes or pastries, in order to gain business from those with higher incomes would have been useful. It would also have been more accurate to discuss falling turnover or sales, rather than profit. **c** The student gives another example of a factor that will influence Warburtons' success, but this time does not get as far as analysis. No connection is pursued to the effect of lower demand on the turnover or sales of the firm. **d** The answer once again reaches Level 3 with some analysis of the effects of health warnings and changing consumer demand on the business's success. Tackling four separate issues in this answer is probably too many. It would have been better to have covered two or three in greater detail. **e** The student achieves Level 4 evaluation by discussing the factor that is most likely to affect the future success of Warburtons and giving the justification for this judgement.

(3) Taxation

Health warnings

New laws affecting the employment of workers

ⓔ **3/3 marks awarded.** The student has stated ways in which the government could affect Warburtons' operation without going into unnecessary detail.

(4) Warburtons may change its objectives in response to the demands of shareholders. **a** They may decide that instead of looking to expand, they want the business to become more cautious, so that profits are protected. **b** As a consequence they may not want to see expansion into new bakeries in new areas.

If the economy looks as if it is going into recession, this might also make shareholders more cautious about the future. They may decide that this is not the time to take risks in moving into new markets and trying to make the firm bigger. They may be happy instead to make sure that profits are maintained rather than risked on new ventures. **c**

ⓔ **7/10 marks awarded.** This question requires Level 3 analysis and an answer that is written in the context of Warburtons. It is also important to remember to give two separate points as requested in the question. **a** The student has started off in context, using evidence from the case study about growth. This is a consideration of growth as an objective, although the student has not discussed it in those terms. **b** The answer goes on to discuss the possible consequences of this change in shareholder attitude. **c** Similarly, the answer looks at the effect of the economy on shareholder objectives for the future. The last sentence of this paragraph would gain low Level 3 marks for analysis.

This answer would have benefited from a more structured discussion of Warburtons' likely objectives in terms of profits, growth and survival. These could then have been linked to factors such as the wishes of the shareholders and the state of the economy. The student could then have discussed the likely result of the change in objectives.

(5) (a) Technology may affect Warburtons in the methods that it uses for stock control. It is important with a perishable product that stock is delivered to the customer as quickly as possible. Effective stock control makes this easier to achieve. **a** They will also be affected by technology in the running of the plant, where computers can control the ingredients going into each loaf and the temperature at which it is cooked. This will make the process more efficient and save money in the long run, although in the short run it will be costly to install. **b**

℮ **4/4 marks awarded.** The student has given two points as the question asks. **a** The first point refers to the need for good stock control in a business producing a perishable good. The point is valid and well made. **b** The second point is also appropriate for a firm like Warburtons. This would be a useful application of technology in improving efficiency.

(5) (b) Profit
Number of employees

℮ **2/2 marks awarded.** Both answers are ways in which the size of a business can be measured.

(5) (c) Warburtons' stakeholders are likely to have different views about the benefits of the new bakery. For the shareholders, this is an opportunity for expansion which has both costs and benefits. In the short term the business will have to find the money to expand, which will either mean extra borrowing or possibly lower dividends. However, the shareholders will hope that in the long term, the expansion will bring extra profits for the firm and the opportunity for them to get higher dividends. **a**

The managers might also have mixed feelings about the expansion. It will make it possible for them to make a success of the venture, which may give them higher salaries or bonuses. It will also help to secure their jobs for the long term. However, it will bring with it extra work and stress as the new business is set up. They will have to hire and train new staff for the bakery and ensure that it is efficient and makes a profit. If they fail in this, the business's profits will suffer and they may put their jobs at risk. **b** It might be difficult to manage this new bakery, given that it is in a completely different part of the country from their traditional locations. They do not know much about operating in the southeast of the UK or about the problems that may arise.

The local community in the new area might also have mixed feelings. The new bakery will bring the prospect of employment, which is likely to be popular at a time when unemployment in the UK is high. It will also mean

problems whilst the factory is being built, and when it starts to operate there will be constant movement of heavy vehicles, bringing in raw materials and taking out deliveries of bread. Many of these deliveries are likely to be during the night, which may create a lot of resistance from local residents. **c**

Overall, I think that stakeholders are more likely to welcome the new bakery and see benefits from it, whether they are shareholders, managers, employees or the local community. There is a lot to be gained for all these groups, especially during a recession. In particular, I think that the new employees at the new factory have most to gain because they will have a job with a successful firm and good prospects for the future. **d**

ⓔ 17/18 marks awarded. This question asks the student to use evaluation to achieve Level 4 marks. The answer also needs to be in context to achieve Level 3 and above. It is important to discuss each stakeholder group by name, rather than referring to stakeholders in general terms. The answer begins by giving evaluative comments. It is not necessary for evaluation always to be at the end of an answer. **a** The student weighs up the cost and benefits for the shareholders in a time-based framework. The answer looks at the short-term costs and weighs them against the likely long-term benefits. **b,c** The student goes on to discuss managers and the local community in a similar way. The answer considers how each of the three groups might gain and lose from the move to London. Although the question does not require a particular number of stakeholders to be discussed, it is always a good idea to discuss at least two stakeholders and not more than three, in detail. Answers that become long lists of every possible stakeholder, but with no analysis of the effects on each one, will only score Level 2 marks, however long they are. **d** The student goes on to give further evaluation by discussing which stakeholder group has most to gain. This answer is evaluative throughout and would score high marks.

ⓔ Total: 53/60 marks — an excellent A grade.

Case study 2 **Innocent shifts its marketing**

1 hour

Innocent is shifting the emphasis of some of its marketing by axing its Village Fête summer event. The business claimed that the savings made would enable it to double its expenditure on highlighting the healthy qualities of its Veg Pots, Smoothies and Squeezies.

The summer fête had replaced Innocent's 'Fruitstock' free music event that had run for 4 years. In its last year, 2000, it attracted over 150,000 people. The Village Fête was held over 2 days in Regent's Park, London, and was publicised as a family event. However, the fête only managed to attract 40,000 people in 2008, although it was suggested that the attendance figures had been hit by rain on the Sunday. Having run 'Fruitstock' for 4 years and the summer fête for 2 years, the company's marketing director, Thomas Delabriere, said that it was time for something else.

Innocent was 10 years old in 2009 and considered it was the right time to change things. In June 2009, the business launched a TV advertising campaign costing £1.2 million. In the same year, Coca-Cola had invested £30 million for around a 10–20% stake in the business.

In September 2011, Innocent introduced an iPhone and iPad app featuring games to enhance the awareness of its Innocent Kids children's drinks.

Sales had declined, possibly partly due to the success of PepsiCo's Tropicana. It was considered that by offering the Veg Pots, Smoothies and Squeezies, Innocent would provide the consumers with fresh value.

Charlotte Highfield, director of the brand consultancy firm Clear stated that if Innocent could own the territory of hassle-free health while maintaining its ethical brand values, it would be able to bring out new products in all areas of food and drink.

In 2011 Innocent added to its product range and spent £2.7 million on a campaign with the strapline, 'here to serve the peckish'.

Some were more concerned about Coca-Cola's investment in Innocent, suggesting that Innocent's unique brand would disappear. However, Thomas Delabriere suggested this would not be an issue, but would provide the company with an alternative source of finance. Whether there would be any conflict between the objectives of Innocent and Coca-Cola would remain to be seen in the future.

In April 2011, Coca-Cola increased its stake in Innocent Smoothies from 18% to 56%.

Sales in 2011 had grown significantly, making Innocent the largest smoothie brand with 75% of the UK market.

Questions

(1) State three stakeholders of Innocent.   (3 marks)

ⓔ The trigger word 'state' requires you just to name or state and nothing more. This is question requires a Level 1 answer and one that ought not to take much time. There is no point in adding additional information as the mark scheme only awards 1 mark for each correctly named stakeholder of Innocent.

(2) (a) Give two examples of market research methods a business like Innocent could use. (2 marks)

(e) This is another question that only requires you to state examples and no more. This can be confusing as students are sometimes unsure about what is meant by 'market research methods'. It is better to state categories rather than giving more specific examples, so a good answer would be desk and field (or secondary and primary) research.

Answers such as questionnaire or interviews may run the risk of not fitting the mark scheme, which is looking for methods and not examples.

(2) (b) Analyse one likely effect of new competition entering the market for 'health drinks'. (6 marks)

(e) The key words in this question are 'analyse' and 'one'. Given the time constraints of this paper, it is important to keep to the requirements of the question.

Another factor to consider is the word 'likely'. Although there is no 'right' answer to this question, some effects are more likely than others. If a student considers an effect that is highly unlikely, the answer is quite likely to receive fewer marks.

**(3) (a) 'Innocent was 10 years old in 2009 and considered it the right time to change things.'
Analyse the way in which stakeholders will be affected by these changes.** (10 marks)

(e) The term 'analyse' immediately informs you that this is a Level 3 question. The question provides a context for the answer ('10 years old…right time to change things').

The question asks you to analyse the ways in which stakeholders (more than one) will be affected. It is important to ensure that you show how particular groups of stakeholders are affected. To do this, it is a good strategy to offer a linked effect and not just state, for example, that a stakeholder 'will get more money'. It is better to show how the additional money is gained and how this actually affects the stakeholder(s), in a positive or negative manner.

The mark allocation is 10 marks and to gain all 10 marks it would be advisable to show how at least two sets of stakeholders will be affected. However, there is no need to show how all stakeholders will be affected, as this would eat into the time allowed to complete the rest of the questions.

**(3) (b) Discuss the ways in which changes in distribution of population in the UK might
affect Innocent's ability to meet its objectives.** (14 marks)

(e) The trigger word 'discuss' immediately informs you that this is a Level 4 question and that evaluative comments are required. The question also states that you are required to discuss 'ways' (more than one) in which the changes affect Innocent's ability to meet its objectives. It is therefore essential that you are able to show how a change will help meet a specific objective rather than talking about the company's objectives in a general manner.

A good answer will show how the changes will affect Innocent's ability to meet specific objectives. Will they make it easier or harder to achieve its objectives, and to what extent?

(4) (a) State three sources of finance that could be used by Innocent.   (3 marks)

ⓔ Remember, this is a 'state' question and therefore you only have to state and no more. There may be a temptation just to list any sources of finance. However, it is important to be mindful of the type of business Innocent is and therefore to state a source of finance that is appropriate for Innocent. The mark scheme will indicate that certain sources of finance are not appropriate for this type of business.

(4) (b) Outline two differences between a public limited company and a private limited company.   (4 marks)

ⓔ This question asks you to 'outline' (give a brief explanation of) two differences — there are no additional marks for outlining three or four.

The question also asks you to show the 'difference' between public and private companies. It is therefore very important for you to show the differences clearly and not leave it to the examiner to work it out. The word 'whereas' is a useful one in helping you to answer this kind of question. An alternative would be to use 'when compared to'.

(5) To what extent might Innocent have benefited from pursuing an ethical stance for the business?   (18 marks)

ⓔ The phrase 'to what extent' is asking you to a make a judgement (Level 4), so it is vital that you do suggest 'to what extent'. Are the benefits significant or are they minor?

Will any benefits be gained immediately or in the long term? Will there be benefits but at a cost to other aspects of the business? Such questions will help you write an appropriate answer.

It is important that you clearly demonstrate how Innocent in particular could benefit from an ethical stance, and do not just make a series of generic points that could apply to any business. Answering in the context of the case remains essential. It is just as legitimate to indicate that Innocent may not benefit and that there may be negative aspects in attempting to be ethical.

Total: 60 marks

Student A

(1) Coca-Cola
Charlotte Highfield, director
Suppliers of Innocent

ⓔ **3/3 marks awarded.** The student has correctly named three stakeholders. Alternatives include the government, the community and shareholders.

(2) (a) Primary (field) research, where information is collected first hand.
Secondary (desk) research, where the information already exists.

ⓔ **2/2 marks awarded.** Although the student has given a correct response, unnecessary additional information has been given. The marks were awarded for primary and secondary; offering even a brief explanation is only wasting valuable time that could be used to tackle the higher-mark questions.

(2) (b)

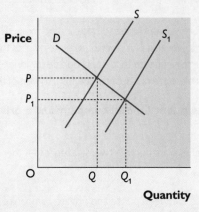

If new competition enters the market for health drinks, the market will get larger (more suppliers), therefore supply will increase, S to S_1. This will lead to a fall in the price level of the market, P to P_1, as firms will lower the prices of their health drinks in order to compete. **a** So consumers have more ability and willingness to buy their drinks rather than those of the competition. **b** Therefore sales and profit will increase. **c** In the long term it is likely firms will be forced out of the market, particularly the smaller less well-established ones as they will not be able to lower their prices as much as larger more established firms whilst protecting their profit margins. **d**

ⓔ **6/6 marks awarded.** The inclusion of a diagram is a quick way in which to gain marks. Drawing the diagram with appropriate labels will gain Level 2 marks and if comments are made on the diagram, it is quite likely that Level 3 marks will be gained. **a** This is a good response and already includes analysis. **b** This is slightly confusing as all companies will be affected by the increased competition unless there is a unique selling point, which means that it is not necessary to lower prices. **c** This comment lacks any explanation or justification. **d** This shows a good insight into possible consequences and is also effective analysis. Once analysis has been demonstrated, the student is scoring either 5 or 6 marks. This student has offered clear analysis in the context of the case and therefore would gain full marks.

(3) (a) Consumers who buy Innocent's products could be both positively and negatively affected by a change in the way it advertised itself and its products. Getting rid of the Village Fête and Fruitstock could change the image of its products. Consumers could benefit from a wider choice of healthy foods and therefore live longer. **a** This would also help the government who are concerned about obesity and the unhealthy food that people are eating. **b** If Innocent changed its approach, with more people eating well the burden on the health service could be less, therefore saving the government money which it could spend on other important areas. **c** However, the local area where the fêtes and Fruitstock were held may suffer as a result of them ending. Local traders who attend the fêtes would lose sales and this may mean that an opportunity to make huge sales in a short period of time is lost.**d**

The shareholders may not be pleased with the changes as the TV campaign is expensive and does not guarantee an increase in sales as it may not reach its target market. This would reduce its profits and therefore the shareholders would get less dividends. **e**

ⓔ **10/10 marks awarded. a** The consumer is an obvious stakeholder and the student states clearly that consumers could be affected in both ways. This statement is then developed successfully. The comments would be viewed as analysis. **b** The student raises another stakeholder and offers a comment as to how it will be affected. However, at this stage, there is a lack of development. **c** This is analysis as there is a clear implication of how the government would be affected. It would have been helpful if the student had suggested a possible area of expenditure that could have been boosted, but the analysis is nevertheless sound. **d** Another stakeholder is considered by the student to good effect, although an implication of the lost sales could have been offered to develop the analysis. **e** This is another Level 3 comment; the consequences for the shareholder are clearly shown.

(3) (b) The changes in the distribution of the population may affect Innocent's ability to meet its objectives in many ways. Firstly, it depends on what the changes in the population are. The size of the population in the UK is increasing and is over 60 million, which is a lot. This means there are more potential customers for Innocent's products and therefore the increase in the population will make it easier for Innocent to achieve its objective of bringing out new products as there will be more to target. **a**

With an increase in the number of old people in the population, healthy drinks may appeal to them to help them stay healthy for even longer and therefore Innocent will again be more likely to be able to achieve its objective of highlighting the healthy qualities of its products. **b** More sales will help spread the cost (economies of scale) of advertising and therefore with lower unit costs Innocent will make more profit and will therefore achieve its objective of being a profitable business. **c**

An increase in the population, however, may stop Innocent achieving its objectives because as the population increases, more firms may want to enter the market and therefore there will be more competition for Innocent, making it harder to make high profits as its prices would have to be competitive and less expensive to ensure it could compete with the new rivals. **d**

How the population actually affects the ability of Innocent to achieve its objectives will depend upon what the actual changes are in the structure of the population and a lot of other factors, **e** so it is difficult to say just how the changes will affect Innocent and to say if the ability to achieve its objectives is due to just the population. Having more potential customers is more likely to help the business. **f**

ⓔ **10/14 marks awarded. a** This is a good attempt at analysis. An implication of the change in demographics is given, although the link to the expected ability of the company to achieve its objectives is rather weak. **b** Again, the student is on the right lines but needs to develop the point in more depth in order to guarantee a Level 3 mark. **c** However, the continuation of the point

in terms of higher sales and the consequences of such sales is a good example of analysis. **d** This is a good example of a negative point, which is presented clearly. There is a clear progression, although the last part of the paragraph is lacking a final comment on which objective would be compromised. **e** It is a pity that the student did not suggest what some of the 'other factors' are. **f** This is more of a summary than an attempt at evaluation, although the student makes a valid attempt to suggest that the effect does depend upon the nature of the actual changes. Where there are several attempts at analysis, it is likely that a Level 3 mark will be awarded.

(4) (a) Bank loan
  Overdraft
  Selling unwanted assets

@ **3/3 marks awarded.** The student has correctly stated three sources of finance. It is important that the sources stated are appropriate for the business in the case.

(4) (b) A public limited company can sell its shares to the public on the stock exchange whereas a private limited company cannot and can only sell to family and employees and not at the stock exchange. **a** A public limited company is usually a larger business than a private limited company, which is probably smaller because it cannot raise as much finance so easily. **b**

@ **4/4 marks awarded. a** The student has clearly outlined the difference in terms of the selling of shares. It is also worth noting that the student has stated what both the public limited company and the private limited company can do, and has not assumed that the examiner knows what the student is thinking. You will not get Level 2 marks if you fail to state what both types of company can or cannot do. **b** Again the student has clearly outlined the differences between the plc and the Ltd.

(5) Innocent may have benefited from pursing an ethical stance as its target audience will have widened. Not only would the business be aiming at consumers that are interested in buying Veg Pots, Smoothies and Squeezies, but Innocent will also be aiming at ethically conscious people who choose what products they buy heavily weighted on ethical issues. **a** With Innocent widening its target audience, more consumers will buy the products of the business and therefore increase the revenue of Innocent. This will allow the business to continue with its growth and expansion which may help Innocent to 'be able to bring out new products in all areas of food and drink'. **b** By being ethical Innocent can increase its customer base and therefore reduce the risk of being reliant on one group of consumers. **c**
Innocent can also benefit by using its ethical stance as a marketing tool. Innocent has changed its marketing, ending the fêtes and having an expensive TV campaign which could feature or include its ethical stance. By doing this Innocent may be able to make its advert appeal to those who are interested in health foods and those who are interested in ethical products. **d** As consumers become more ethical in their outlook, Innocent may be seen as a forward-thinking business and therefore attract further customers which will lead to higher sales, higher revenue and therefore higher profits. **e** This will please its shareholders and its new partner Coca-Cola which may therefore be prepared to invest more into the

business. A profitable business will find it easier to gain loans from banks as it will appear healthier, and this extra finance will allow it to expand and be competitive. It may also mean that Innocent does not need to rely on Coca-Cola to invest more and take a greater share in the business, which will be a benefit to Innocent as it can do its own thing and not have to do things the Coca-Cola way. This will reduce the possible conflict in objectives between the two businesses. **f**

The most important factor and benefit for Innocent of being ethical is the competitive edge that it may bring. Innocent is not relying on just its products, even though they are seen as unique. Its ethical stance is an additional benefit because in today's competitive markets if a product has two good features this is better than just having one. **g**

e **16/18 marks awarded. a** This is a good start and would be a Level 2 response. There is no development or implication for the business at this stage. **b** This is analysis; there is an implication for the business in the context of the case. **c** This is an additional implication which enhances the analysis already highlighted. **d** This comment is the start of a possible valid piece of analysis; however, at this stage it is only a Level 2 comment. This is because there is no obvious implication for Innocent. Having stated that the ethical stance can be used as a marketing tool, the student does not offer any implication of this in terms of sales, revenue or share of the market. **e** This is clearly a Level 3 response. The point is made and the implication follows in an effective manner. **f** This another effective piece of analysis. The contextual reference is particularly strong and relevant. **g** The answer finishes with an evaluative point. The student makes a judgement about which is the most important benefit, and this is also justified. Although further justification could have been offered, a Level 4 mark would be awarded.

e **Total: 54/60 — an impressive A grade.**

Student B

(1) Employees
     Shareholders
     Suppliers

e 3/3 marks awarded. The student has listed three stakeholder groups.

(2) (a) Questionnaire in the street
        Postal questionnaire

e 2/2 marks awarded. The student has stated two examples of primary research.

(2) (b) If a new competitor enters the market for health drinks, Innocent might find that the demand for their products is falling. **a** Innocent might need to take action to ensure that they can stop this happening. One thing they could do is to undertake a new advertising campaign in the media. This could be combined with a special offer promotion to make it more successful. **b** In doing this Innocent would hope that they could increase the demand for their products and maintain turnover. **c**

ⓔ 5/6 marks awarded. a The student has begun by giving the likely effect of a new competitor entering the market. **b** The answer has then gone on to explain how Innocent might react to this threat and **c** has finally explained the reason for this action. The last two points have used analysis in explaining the effects on Innocent, so Level 3 is achieved.

(3) (a) If Innocent decides to change its method of operations, a number of stakeholders will be affected. It may be necessary for working practices to change to take account of something like new technology. This will mean that workers need to be trained in new techniques and also that they have to be willing to accept changes to the way they work. The employees may be resistant to these changes. However, if they do not accept them, the business may struggle and their jobs may be put at risk in the future. **a**

Shareholders may have to find the money for any changes through being prepared to accept lower dividends. This is not usually popular with shareholders because they are not guaranteed that the changes will be successful. The hope for the shareholders will be that the changes lead to higher profit and more dividends in the long run. **b**

ⓔ 8/10 marks awarded. This question requires the student to analyse the effects of making changes. In this case the student has looked at two stakeholder groups. It is important that stakeholders are identified by name. **a** The student has considered the effect on the employees of any change and their response to it. The answer then goes on to analyse the implications of those changes for employees. **b** The student analyses the costs and benefits for the shareholders of making changes to the business.

(3) (b) Population distribution can change in a number of different ways. It can change geographically as people move around the country. The age distribution may also change. **a**

Population movements can affect Innocent in terms of the production and distribution of its products. Most of what Innocent produces has a fairly short life or needs to be kept refrigerated. If people start to move to live in different areas this may affect Innocent's production and distribution costs and reduce its profits. If Innocent has set an objective like 5% growth a year for the next 3 years, it might find itself struggling to meet this target when costs increase. **b**

Changes in age distribution could have big implications for Innocent meeting its objectives if those include improvements in profitability or growth for the future. **c** At the moment most of Innocent's market is amongst young, health conscious adults with a good standard of living. Their products are not cheap and they are sold mainly as healthy options. If the UK population continues to age in terms of its distribution, Innocent could find that its target market is shrinking and that it needs to look for new groups of consumers to sell to. **d** This could mean falling sales and profits unless the firm can successfully find new markets. Even that will cost them money though, in market research and advertising. This could mean that Innocent fails to meet any objectives it has set itself.

In the same way, the recession could stop the firm achieving its objectives. Innocent's products are not essential and they are expensive in relation to other soft drinks. Falling incomes would have a big impact on any growth or profit objectives. **e**

Overall I think that changes in the age distribution will have the biggest effect because Innocent is aimed at a young sector of the population. However, if Innocent can get some brand loyalty in this sector of the population, maybe these young people will continue to buy Innocent products and it will then be possible to achieve objectives. **f**

ⓔ **12/14 marks awarded. a** The student begins by showing understanding of the meaning of population distribution to achieve Level 1 marks. **b** The answer then shows how population distribution might have an effect on Innocent's objectives by considering and naming what those objectives are likely to be. **c,d** The student then takes two specific examples of changes in population distribution — geographical and age. In each case, an explanation is given of how this change might have an impact on Innocent reaching its objectives, and it links through from sales to profit implications. **e** This shows analysis and would take the answer to Level 3. In this answer, two effects analysed in depth are sufficient. **f** The answer finishes by evaluating which of the changes is likely to have more impact on Innocent's ability to reach its objectives.

(4) (a) Bank loan
Overdraft
Leasing equipment instead of buying

ⓔ **3/3 marks awarded.** The student has stated three acceptable sources of finance.

(4) (b) A public limited company will have the letters plc after its name. A private limited company will have Ltd after its name. A public limited company can sell its shares on the Stock Exchange. A private limited company must make a personal approach to friends, family or employees if it wants to sell shares.

ⓔ **4/4 marks awarded.** Students often confuse public and private companies with the public and private sector. They also tend to write complicated and confused answers to this question. This answer shows that it is possible to give a fairly simple response and still achieve full marks. Two differences between public and private companies have been explained clearly.

(5) Ethical behaviour has become increasingly important for businesses in modern society. Consumers are now interested to know how a firm behaves, how it produces its products and treats its staff. Innocent has marketed itself as an ethical business. **a**

Innocent has decided that it will produce its drinks using natural products and without additives to differentiate itself from its competitors. The soft drinks market is huge, with many different companies producing in it. Some of these companies, like Coca-Cola, are multinational with large economies of scale.

Innocent would never be able to compete with a business like this. Instead they have looked for a niche in the market where there are fewer competitors. **b** As a result they have built up a market of customers who want to buy healthy and natural drinks.

The benefits of all this for Innocent are that their name is now recognised as a product which is healthy and ethically produced. This gives Innocent the opportunity to charge higher prices than companies not following the same strategy. **c** Customers who want ethically produced goods are usually prepared to pay more for them. This should mean that Innocent's profits increase as the demand for their product rises.

On the other hand, the current recession has shown that when things get difficult consumers stop buying these more expensive products and look for cheaper products to lower their spending. **d** This means that Innocent's ethical stance may put it at risk in the current economic climate.

There is also a risk of new competition entering a niche market. Innocent produces on quite a small scale so other competitors may see their profits and try to come into the market. This could also affect Innocent's future sales and profitability. **e**

Overall, Innocent has probably gained by setting itself up as an ethical business. It has differentiated itself from the competition and stuck to its principles. However, it may find it difficult to stick to these principles if the recession continues. **f**

ⓔ 15/18 marks awarded. **a** The answer starts by showing that the student understands why businesses might pursue an ethical policy. It explains the benefits for the firm. **b** The student then gives specific benefits for Innocent. The answer discusses the benefits in terms of sales, achieving Level 2. **c** The answer then goes on to achieve Level 3 marks by explaining these benefits in more detail, looking at the possibilities for charging higher prices for an ethical product. **d,e** The answer begins evaluation by weighing up the possible problems associated with this ethical stance. The student looks at the risks in a niche market and the effects of the recession. **f** The student then reaches a conclusion which is important in a question that asks 'to what extent'. The answer says that it will depend on what happens in the future, but it is an attempt to answer the question specifically as it is set.

ⓔ **Total: 52/60 marks — a good A grade.**

Knowledge check answers

1 Constraints include: competition, legislation, economy, taxation, inflation, social and environmental issues.

2 The state may act as a consumer, supplier and regulator.

3 Stakeholders who may be in conflict include: employees and trade unions, employers, shareholders and customers.

4 Likely essential resources include: business plan, finance, employees, right or unique product or service.

5 Reasons include: a poor business plan or no business plan; a lack of, or no, professional advice; a lack of market research; an inability to change with the times; a poor product or service; and an inability to grow.

6 Working capital is used for buying raw materials, paying wages, paying utility bills and marketing.

7 The main difference is that for leasing the consumer does not own the good.

8 A hotel is labour intensive; a car factory is capital intensive.

9 Items listed within a person profile may include: qualifications, experience, specific qualities such as an ability to motivate others, good ICT skills.

10 By offering free samples to the loyalty card holders of a supermarket, running a focus group, employing a market research company to undertake a survey.

11 Possible methods include: considering the competition by looking in *Yellow Pages*; using existing research.

12 Possible methods include: ask every fifth person coming into the gym; deliver a questionnaire to homes in the area of the gym; phone/text a random selection of gym members.

13 Possible answers include:
- Primary: extraction of raw materials, e.g. coalmining, drilling for oil.
- Secondary: manufacture of products, e.g. a car plant, building houses.
- Tertiary: service, e.g. supermarkets, hairdressers, advertising, banking.

14 A deed of partnership is useful because it allows partners to know: how much profit each takes out; how responsibilities are shared; the arrangements for absence and sickness; how decisions will be made; how new partners will be chosen and employed; how the partnership will be dissolved.

15 Benefits include: cheaper initial outlay; marketing undertaken by franchisor; established brand; brand name; less risk; expert help available.

16 The size of a travel agency could be measured by the number of outlets, its turnover, or the number of employees.

17 A mission statement is a general statement which sets out the purpose of the business. An objective is a specific goal.

18 Tactical objectives are short term, set and carried out by junior managers; they affect a particular department of the business not the firm as a whole. Strategic objectives are long term, set and implemented by senior managers; they usually affect the whole business.

19 Internal constraints arise from within the business, e.g. poor communication. External constraints arise from the environment in which the firm operates, e.g. the state of the economy.

20 The community in which a business operates is treated as a stakeholder and so social objectives (e.g. the reduction of waste and sourcing a certain percentage of products locally) are set to reflect this.

21 Demand and supply.

22 A competitive market has many firms, an oligopoly has a few large dominant firms, and (in theory) a monopoly only has one firm. In practice in the UK a monopoly is said to exist when a business controls 25% of the market.

23 Productivity is output per person in a particular period of time — usually an hour. Efficiency is a related concept that considers outputs relative to inputs; a firm that has become 'more efficient' produces the same (or more) output with fewer inputs.

24 Possible answers include:
- Different demographic groups in the population demand different products, e.g. 'the grey economy' is very different from the teenage market.
- Different demographic groups have to be targeted by specific types of advertising and promotional offers.
- Changes in demographics can lead to skill shortages and therefore there are training implications.
- Employment practices may have to change, e.g. recognition that it will now be necessary to employ more older employees.
- Pension implications. If a firm's ex-employees are going to live for longer, more funds will have to be set aside for payments to be made in their retirement. There is obviously an opportunity cost to this.

25 Laws lay down what a business must do; they are minimum standards to be adhered to. Failure to comply is illegal and renders a firm liable to prosecution. Unethical behaviour (such as obtaining products made using child labour in a less developed country) does not break UK law, although it may well be regarded as wrong by many.

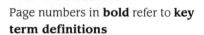

Page numbers in **bold** refer to **key term definitions**

A

adding value   9

advertising and promotion   39

ageing population   46

aims/goals   33

appointment of employees   20

aptitude testing   20

Articles of Association   29

assets   32

B

balance of payments   9, 11

breaking even   33

business

   classification of   26–32

   functions of   8

   purposes of   9

   role of   7–9

   success/failure   14–15, 56

business angels   18

business markets   7

business plans   **13**

business resources   13–15

C

capital   7, 8, 55

capital employed   32

capital equipment   **15**

cluster sampling   24

collusion   44

community   11, 48

competition   8, 66

competitive markets   43

competitive supply   41

competitors   23

complementary goods   40

constraints   8, 34

consumer durables   7

consumer non-durables   7

contracts of employment   20

convenience sampling   24

corporate social responsibility
   (CSR)   **49**–50

costs   40

customer data   23

customers   10

CVs   20

D

decision making   34

deed of partnership   27–28

deindustrialisation   26

demand   **37**, 39–40, 41,
   42–43, 47

demand curve   37, 39

demand schedule   37

demographic changes   40

demography   **46**

dividends   17

E

e-business   30

economy   8, 26

elasticity   42–43

employees   10, 13–14, 31, 48

employment   9, 11, 47

enterprise   7

environmental issues   9

equilibrium price   38–39, 41, 42

essential resources   13–14

ethical behaviour   **48**–50, 67

external constraints   **34**

external finance   16

F

factoring   16

factors of production   55

finance   8, 14, 15–18, 67

franchises   29

G

government   11–12, 40, 56

government data   23

government grants   18

growth   33

H

hire purchase   17

human resources management
   (HRM)   8, 18–22

I

income   39

incorporation   28

induction of employees   21

industry   7

inflation   9

Innocent   65–74

inputs   **7**

internal constraints   **34**

internal finance   16

internet data   23

interview panels   20

interviews

   job   20

   market research   22

J

job adverts   19–20

job descriptions   19, 20

job selection process   20

job specifications   19, 20

L

labour   7, 19

labour/capital intensive
   firms   **19**

land   7

leasing   17

legislation   8

lenders   11

limited companies   28–29

limited liability   28

limited liability partnerships
   (LLPs)   29

loans   11

long-term finance   17

long-term loans   17

M

managers   13–14

marketing   8

market research   22–23, 55–56,
   66

market research data   23

markets   7, **36**–44

market share   33

medium-term finance   17

medium-term loans   17

Memorandum of Association   29

merit goods   12

microeconomics   36

mission statements   33

monopolies   43–44

mortgages   17

N

nationalisation   30

newspapers and magazines   23

O

objectives   33–36, 56

observations   23

off-the-job training   21

oligopolies   44

on-the-job training   21

opportunity cost   34

outputs   **7**

overdrafts   16

owners   10

P

partnerships   27–28

person profiles   19, 20

population   46–47, 66

price   36–39, 40

price elasticity   **42**

primary data   22

primary research   22–23

primary sector   26, 45

private limited companies   28, 67

private sector businesses   27–29

privatisation   30

production   8, 26

productivity   **45**

products   14

profit   31, 33

psychometric tests   20

public limited companies   28–29,
   67

public sector businesses   27,
   29–30

Q

qualitative market research   22

quantitative market research   22

questionnaires   22

quota sampling   25

R

random sampling   24

recruitment   19

regulation   12

retained profits   17

revenue   9

S

sales figures   23

sampling   24–25

secondary data   22

secondary research   23

secondary sector   26, 45

sectors of economy   26

services   7, 14

shareholders   10

shares   17, 28, 31

short-term finance   16

short-term loans   16

size of business   31–32, 57

SMART objectives   34

social benefits   11

social costs   11

social demographics   46–47

social issues   9

social objectives   35

sole traders   27

stages of production   26

stakeholders   9–13, 49, 57, 65, 66

state   12

Stock Exchange   28, 31

stock market value   31

strategic objectives   33

stratified sampling   24

subsidies   40

substitutes   40

suppliers   11, 48

supply   **37**, 40–41, 42, 43

supply curve   37–38, 40

supply schedule   37–38

surveys   22

survival   33

SWOT analysis   **35**

systematic sampling   24

T

tactical objectives   33–34

tastes and fashion   39

taxation   8–9, 11, 40

technology   45, 57

tertiary sector   26, 45

test panels   23

trade credit   16

trade publications   23

training   21

turnover   31

V

venture capitalists   18

W

Warburtons   55–64

wealth   39

weather   41

working capital   8, 15

OCR AS Business Studies